Become

Hidden Treasures in Earthen Vessels

By

Hellen A. Nkwocha

Editor's Note: You will find at the back of the book notes with Scripture references used. Unless otherwise indicated, all Scripture quotations are from the Holy Bible: New International Version (NIV).

Notes on quotes: except otherwise specified, all the quotes cited are retrieved from Everyday Power.

queentavisuals@yahoomail.com

ISBN book 978 94 6466 570 3

ISBN e-book 978 94 64 66 57 10

A book that sways from an autobiography to a work that transverses two continents as a young girl does a socio psychological analysis of her journey to Become an accomplished woman. Deeply inspirational and highly educative.

- Mr. Chris Dahi

Author of the book "Bonded", and others.

"A bird doesn't sing because it has an answer, it sings because it has a song."

— Maya Angelou

This book is dedicated to all aspiring to Become and to unleash the greatness within.

ACKNOWLEDEMENTS

No man is an island and no one person has it all. The realization of this book would not have been possible without the inspiration and the assistance of very special people in my life.

My special thanks and gratitude go to all the great leaders who have inspired me with their words and lifestyle.

My deep gratitude goes to my spiritual parents, Pastor Mike, and Pastor Mrs. Boma Nwanegbo, for their support, prayers, and belief in me.

To my meticulous editors, proofreaders and dear friends, Mrs. Nicoline Mbah, Mrs. Janée Angel, Mr. Chris Dahi, Queenta Ambrose and all who contributed in one way or the other to the success of this book, I say thank you for your sincere and critical reviews and assistance, words cannot express my gratitude.

To my lovely family: my dear husband, Kingsley, and children, Micayla, Gloria and Michael, you are my motivation. You give me wings to fly. THANK YOU for having this unwavering belief in me. I love you all!

Finally, to the One with whom all things are possible, my Maker, My Owner, because He is, I am. I am forever grateful!

Table of Contents

FOREWORD

We are beings made in the image of God but resides in a vessel of clay. Who we are is not the physical body but the personality resident in the body. We are not ordinary and every human is a carrier of great heavenly treasure with the purpose of achieving a set goal on earth. Life itself is a treasure and the realization of this truth is all you need to become.

So many people in this world have allowed circumstances to determine their destinies or what they think about themselves. Rev. Jessy Jackson said that he was born in the slum but the slum was not born in him.

Mrs Hellen Ayaa Nkwocha has done a good job here by telling us the story of her life and the obstacles that she went through. She was abused, neglected, rejected yet she refused to be written off. She recognized the treasure in her and was determined to manifest the treasure than become what the world had projected her to become. She was not ashamed to tell her story. It is a practical presentation of what most people go through in life. Many have died without becoming what they were created to become.

The process of becoming must be pursued with focus and tenacity. Societal pressure must be ignored.

Remember that you are a hidden treasure in an earthen vessel. It is time to begin manifesting the treasure in you.

This book is a must read. It will change your life for the best.

- Pastor Mike Chuks Nwanegbo

Senior Pastor of New Life International Church.

(RCCG) Antwerp, Belgium

PREFACE

"Until the lion learns to write for himself, the narrative will always favor the hunter."

- Dr. Myles Munroe

It is not a secret that stories are told from the writer's point of view. The writer writes whatever he or she perceives to be worth writing and therefore, the truth of a situation. Histories are written from the perspective of the perceived victors and orators.

News is framed in a way to attract and appeal to the public. In most cases, this results in a single-sided story. A lot gets lost in this single-sided view because we don't get to read the complete story. Chimamanda Ngozi Adichie explained in a TED-Talk the danger of a single story. A single-sided story, especially the one written about you, is a shadow of the real you. It is told each time from the narrator's point of view, who might omit, forget, or add some parts to it.

There are many sides to a story and only you have the full picture of your life's story, so therefore, only you can write the story you want people to read about you. Any attempt by someone else will only portray the idea of who you are and not the essence of the real you.

This book is an attempt to help you become the master and owner of your own story. Everyone, including you, is a special gift to creation. You have something that we all need and stories yet untold. You carry the solution to a problem and you may not even be aware of this. It might sound flattery, but this is a hard truth. You might have heard countless times that you are nothing, or you have been regarded as being useless and so you may have concluded based on your present circumstances or your past events that what they say about you is true.

There is no one without a history. Everyone is given the equal opportunity in life called today and tomorrow which holds its promises. Only you can determine how tomorrow will look like by the choices you make in your today without looking back to your past. The way is forward, not backward. Looking backward should only be done for the sole purpose of understanding your today and amending things for a better tomorrow. You are the architect, the decorator, and the executor of your life through the choices you make. Don't get me wrong, I am not denying the fact that there are other factors in play in the journey of life.

Nevertheless, you have the ultimate key called choice. To some, this is a liberation, while to others, it is a suffocating thought. It all depends on your knowledge of things and how you understand them. Your mindset towards life will ultimately determine the outcome for you.

I invite you to read further into this book as I take you on a journey of self-discovery and problems solving, even as I narrate my story and the things helping me in my process to BECOME.

Hellen A. Nkwocha

INTRODUCTION

BECOME is a topic so dear to my heart because it is a process that only ends with life itself. I desire to inspire, motivate, and encourage everyone reading this book to become who they have been destined to be.

Everyone has a place and a role to play in this life. I call life a journey because that is what it is. We are on a journey with a beginning and an ending. Like an architect who first envisions, then designs every inch of a project before handing it over to the builders to build, so also our lives are envisioned and designed by the greatest Architect of all time and handed over to us. We hereby become the builders and the drivers of this journey. Whether we will reach our destination depends on us and the choices we make along the way. The key to Becoming is in your hands. This book aims to help you see some truths and help you identify things in your life that might either be a stumbling block or a contributor to your progress.

This book does not pretend to hold all the answers to the question of who you are, nor have any new theories, as there is nothing new under the sun. It is, however, an attempt to make you see things differently from a different perspective.

The book is divided into three parts. Part one deals with the issue of who you are. This part, like all other parts, is narrated from my own experiences and what has helped me to identify who I am. The question of who you are is personal and as you will read, you will realize that only YOU can give an answer to this question. Part two deals with the issue of emotions and their role in the process of becoming. Emotions are powerful as we all know, and they have significant impact on our lives. Part three, which is the final part, deals with vision, purpose, and the importance of strategy in the whole process. Strategies are the technics, tactics, and mechanisms that can be activated or used to get the desired results.

You cannot Become without knowing who you are, without being aware of the emotions controlling you, and without building a strong vision that transcends your today.

PART ONE: WHO ARE YOU?

Have you ever been asked this question: *"Who are you?"* A question frequently asked by many people, and probably, you have also asked other people this question. Have you paused and pondered on the answer you want to receive through this question? Is it the name of the person you are interested in knowing? Or is your interest in where he or she lives? Or is it just a rhetoric question demanding no answer?

This is a profound question that has kept many great minds busy till date. Many have tried to answer it to their understanding. However, this question can only be answered by no other person than yourself.

A possible way to look at this question is like the French philosopher, E. Descartes who said, *"Je pense donc je suis,"* meaning, I think therefore I am. But then another question emerges from this stream of thought, which is, *'what do you think and how do you think?'* Since to know who you are you need to have an idea of who you are, then you need to know how and what you think about yourself. To know how you think about yourself, it requires a deep search within you as you look back into the past and if possible and preferable, a glimpse into the future.

This part of the book does not pretend to have the answer to this profound question. It is however an invitation to search within yourself in order to unlock some deep-seated secrets that might be holding the answers from where the journey of self-discovery can start. I invite you to follow me as I reveal my secrets, as I have and still walking the path of deep searching in my process to Become.

1. Defiled, But Undefined

"I know what I want, I have a goal, an opinion, I have a religion and love. Let me be myself and then I will be satisfied. I know that I am a woman, a woman with inward strength and plenty of courage."

– Anne Frank

My life has been one of many colors and shades. I was born and raised till my teenage years in Accra, the capital City of Ghana in West Africa. I was born as an only child, but nevertheless, I was not alone. My mother, being the eldest of her siblings, was encumbered with the family burden of taking care of her siblings as it is the custom in most parts of Africa. My mother held a job as a prison officer and through this job we were offered a house in the government-provided housing for prison officers. In Ghana, all government officers have their barracks. There is the police barrack, the prison officers' barrack, the army barrack, and so on. The type of housing an officer gets depends on the ranking and the duties. Thus, we had a room in one of the housing blocks for normal officers. I call it a room because this is what it was: a one-room house which was partitioned with furnitures and curtains into a living room and a bedroom. The bathroom, toilet and kitchen were in separate units and were shared by two families. We lived there with five other people. My father wasn't living with us because he had travelled out of the country.

My life then was mixed with secrets and shameful wounds on one hand, and real genuine happiness on the other hand. It was difficult for me to comprehend how I could be happy in a moment and the next moment I would feel lost. It felt like living in two worlds at the same time. Have you ever felt like that?

I took life as it came and as an only child, I felt the burden of the need to always maintain a good behavior, not to disappoint my family, always trying to seek the approval

of people around me, though somehow, I still failed to

keep up to these standards. I realized that pleasing people was a full-time job on its own; it was and never would be enough. I had, nevertheless, some good laughs with the kids in the hood. We always knew how to catch fun. Every Sunday we would gather together to go to the Sunday School in a nearby school to study the Bible. That, and dancing were some of my favorite activities of the week. I felt at peace during those moments. It looked as though I had no problem.

HIDDEN WOUNDS AND WORDS

Those peaceful moments were constantly interrupted with moments of pain and sorrow. This part will come as a surprise to those that knew me then because I had mastered the art of concealing my pains at a very young age. It was as if my life was this big stage, where I would put up a mask suitable for any occasion, burying pains and wounds so deep that they seemed unreachable.

I never understood why and how a child could develop these forms of defense mechanisms without being taught explicitly. Is it our survival instincts that kicks in and take over? Is it a deliberate attempt to forget and escape reality even as we live in this reality? Or is it the result of the unwritten rules of engagement of the society we find ourselves in?

Back to my story. I was never alone because I had other family members at home and at any given time. Yet, there were many times I felt completely lost and all alone. This was due to the silent sufferings I was enduring. With all the eyes around me, none could see what was going on. One of the neighbors, who was also a family friend, was sexually preying on me. This man and his wife were both prison officers. He however had a separate duty, which was that he was a member of the music band. Because of this, he was given an apartment in the housing block specially reserved for members of the music band. We lived in the same housing block with his wife and children, so he had the luxury of entering the houses as he deemed fit.

For as long as I can remember, this mas used to sexually abuse me, in broad daylight despite the presence of people all over the place, both in his apartment and in his wife's apartment. At that time, he was one of the few people with colored television, and that is what he used most of the time to lure us. As children, we would be so excited when he invited us to come and watch TV at his apartment. I mostly ended up sleeping over there, because he usually refused to walk us back home in the dark. In the night, he would carry me over to his bed, put a pillow under me and force his way into me while covering my mouth from the painful sounds. This also went on during the daytime. He would call me with the pretense that he wanted me to go and buy something like groundnut for him. If I dared to decline his call or try to be stubborn, the adults around will insult me for not being obedient. I would be left with no choice but to comply.

The pains were unbearable. I had wounds in my private parts most of the time that just urinating was a terrifying ordeal. Most of the time, I felt like I was being swallowed up by a giant big-bellied monster, who, after has had enough of me, vomits me back. This made me felt so dirty and sick each time I came out of his presence. To avoid feeling this way, I created an alternative world I would run to each time I felt swallowed up.

I will explain more about this coping mechanism below.

This abuse persisted for some years. Because of this, I preferred to walk the streets just to be out of his reach. I had no one to turn to or share my pains with. I also had the impression that talking about issues like this was not done, because during that time, I never heard of anything like that. My aunties thought I was being stubborn and lazy because I would run out to the streets in the slightest opportunity. They called me all sorts of names, thinking that I was only being obstinate. I didn't know how to explain my plight to them because I thought they could see what was happening to me. Thus, I went on putting on masks to cover my pains and shame as though it was required of me.

TRANSFER AND TRANSITION

After a while, my mother was transferred to a different city. I was attending an American Baptist school, which was considered as a prestigious school. In order for me

not to lose my status in this school, my mother sent me to live with my uncle, one of my father's brothers, who was a police officer. He lived in a similar flat as ours with his wife and three children. I became the third wheel in this family and thus did not fit in. I lived in a constant state of anxiety, not knowing when I would do something wrong or why I was always doing something wrong. I was beaten for almost everything in addition to my daily house chores. There were some days I was deprived of food as part of a punishment.

As a child, I used to bed-wet. This had been an issue for as long as I could remember. This problem was like a curse to me, and the reason why all that was happening to me was justified. While living with my uncle, each time I would bed-wet, almost the whole neighborhood would hear about it. I was probably seven years of age at that time. I lived for approximately two years with them. There was not a day I did not wish never to have been born. I questioned even at that tender age the very purpose of my existence. What good had life to offer, and what would become of me since I was classified as useless? I also used to see myself as an orphan, I had no one to fight for or care for me. I used to question God on why He would allow all that to happen to me and not do anything about it. What good was all that suffering for or did I do something worth that punishment? I cried myself to sleep almost every night asking God to forgive me and take away my life.

I wasn't allowed to go to church or even attend Sunday schools while I was living with my uncle. Yet, I would sneak out of the house at the slightest chance to go to the nearby church building to cry out to God and sometimes, to just be there. I was often beaten as a punishment for my disobedience, but despite the beatings, I could not stop going to the church building. I did this because there was always the feeling of peace I experienced each time I was inside the church. I felt that there was hope and even though I did not understand what was going on, I used to tell God that even if He had abandoned me, I have not, because I had no one else to turn to.

The transition from my mother's house to my uncle's was obvious even to people who weren't related to me. The neighbors saw and often commented on some of the maltreatment I endured, but they did nothing to help me. The only way some of them could show their concern, was to give me food secretly when I had no food. My school authorities also saw that something wasn't right. My uniforms were always unkept, and I had no lunchbox or money for lunch. The school used to give free lunch towards the school's closing time, and I would eat as much as I could get, that I was nicknamed "*foodian*" and "*Russian tanker,*" because I ate in anticipation of what I might face at home. That food was usually my first meal of the day and often my only meal.

After living with my uncle and his family for about two years, I asked my mother to allow me come home for holiday at where she was living and she agreed. Luckily, there were also some changes in the school which was a blessing to me. The school's bus driver was going on retirement, and as the school did not have any trusted driver to replace him, the school bus was abandoned till further notice. Students were asked to cater for their transportation. This news was a blessing to me because it meant that my mother needed to hire a taxi to pick me up from home to school and vice versa every day. That act implied an increase in the cost of transportation, an expense we couldn't afford at that time. Hence, my mother decided to let me stay with her and attend the nearby school. It was and still is a private school with a combined system of day students and boarding students.

As fate would have it, after almost a year of attending the school as a day student, my mother was transferred back to where we came from, in fact, to the very apartment block I used to live in before. My mother decided that it would be better for me to attend a boarding school so that my education would not be confused. So, I became a *"boarder,"* as we used to call it (meaning that I lived inside the school without going home).

I went home only on vacations, and unfortunately, that same man who used to molest me was never transferred to another barrack, so he continued from where he stopped. I was crippled with fear, unable to stop it or to say anything. I could see myself shouting out for help, but my voice was never heard. Life seemed unfair and unreasonable. My only escape was the strolling I used to take with Skippy through the blocks. Skippy was my first pet dog and best friend. We were inseparable most of the time whenever I was home from school. It was unusual at that time to have a dog as a pet, especially in that kind of housing. All the neighboring children became Skippy's friend and my friends too. I kept myself busy with all kinds of activities so that I wouldn't have any lonely moments to think or feel anything. The moments with Skippy were very special to me, they helped me live like a child and to play free of worries.

In the boarding school, I grew more matured in my understanding of the issues of life. I came to understand that you either become a lion or be eaten up. It was at this point I came to realize what this man was doing to me. An incident occurred where one of my teachers was raping some of the pupils. That was the first time I heard the word 'rape' and associated it with my own experiences. I also realized that whatever was happening to me was not my fault; it was out of the selfish and evil desires of a derailed man. From that moment, my resistance and stubbornness towards this mas grew the more. I would decline to his calls, even when I got yelled at, I cared less about the consequences. He would sometimes beat me publicly with the excuse that I insulted or disobeyed him. It was common at that time for an adult who is not a parent of a child to discipline that child when it was needed. After seeing the change in me and my refusal to comply and to remain silent, he finally backed off. I was about eleven years of age at that time. My family, friends and neighbors were still seemingly clueless to all that was going on.

For the first time in my childhood life, I felt I could breathe in a way I had never done before. I felt empowered and at the same time stupid. Why did I allow all that to happen if I could stop this man with threats?

How would I have known when the seed of fear, of complying, and of concealing had already been sown in me even before I was aware of them? Who was mentoring me to let me know and see the truth?

MONSTERS WITHIN

There are some wounds we bury so deep within us. We usually hope that by so doing they will somehow disappear or will lose their grip on us. These wounds somehow become a different creature within us, a devouring monster, silently killing us from within. We spend time running away from problems we cannot escape from and all it seems to do is grow larger under the shadows.

There are words unspoken, lying dormant within us, trying to get our attention, but don't seem to get through the thickness of the overwhelming monster of our wounds. Words we are either ashamed of or too fearful to speak out because of their perceived threats. We keep running but can't find any refuge or resting place. However, the question we should ask ourselves is, "how long will we remain a fugitive to ourselves?" I kept running from the pains of these words and my wounds, and from their perceived threats to my very existence. I thought speaking out would be more painful, too shameful and will make me a social pariah.

There seemed also to be no safe place to utter these hurts. Many people look in the mirror of themselves but see only the pains and not the healing possibilities, because they have never been taught on how or what to look for. They see the growing dark shadow of themselves and not the liberating and illuminating truth in the hidden words. Like I said earlier, I was once like that. I found my liberation as I spoke out after a long time and faced the wounds head on. This liberation happened during my university years. I had to go through this process alone which was not easy. Maybe if I had a safe place earlier in life, it would have helped me to come out of the shadows quicker.

Children adapt to their environment as they see them. With no proper guidelines on how to interpret situations and on how these relates to them, they fill in the blanks to their best abilities. They go into adulthood with these coping mechanisms, and if they are not strong enough or if they do not have the necessary help and support, they hardly find the way to knowing who they are.

There is more to a behavior than what the eye can see. If you have been through similar circumstances, you can relate to what I am talking about. Even if you have not, it is very important we have our eyes and ears open for our surroundings and can be that listening ear or that shoulder to lean on for another who desperately needs it.

It was after I was able to confront my hidden wounds, I was able to see the possibilities and the reason why I am here. That is when I realized the truth: Yes, I was defiled, my innocence was stolen from me, but I am undefined by them and my Creator did not and has not abandoned me.

What is your truth?

2. Above All Circumstances

"I love the man that can smile in trouble, that can gather strength from distress and grow brave by reflections."

- Thomas Paine

We often don't choose our circumstances, but we can choose how to respond or deal with them. All that happened to me as a child was not by my choice or doing, neither did I deserved them. They happened because some people choose to afflict such pain on a defenseless girl. Even now as an adult, there are some circumstances I have no control over. Your situation might be different from my own, but nevertheless,

we all have a choice to make in every given circumstance. This might sound contradictory, but it is
however, not the case. We don't have control over the choices of other people, the only control we have, is that of our own choices, because they eventually determine our future.

The ability to see and make our choices is influenced by different factors; they are influenced by our character, our upbringing, our circumstances, our beliefs, our education, and the people we associate with and listen to. However, there is a constant factor in all of these, which is our choice is something that must come from within ourselves no matter the reason.

NATURE VS. NURTURE

For a long time, there has been debates and experiments on what influences humans the most;

Nature or Nurture. Different philosophers have given their opinion
concerning this topic and still do today. For example, Jean-Jacque Rousseau and John Locke, two opposing philosophers.

Jean-Jacque Rousseau was a French philosopher who wrote on different topics, including the nature-nurture debate. He believed that as individuals, we are solely determined by what we inherit from our parents, that is, genetics. According to him, the environment, is not a determinant factor or an active contributor to who we become, because its purpose is to create conducive circumstances to aid an individual become.

On the other hand, we have John Locke, an English philosopher, who also researched, amongst others, this nature-nurture debate. He believed that we are all born blank, we are all born with nothing, a term referred to as *"Tabula rasa,"* meaning clean-sheet. According to his theory, we as individuals are born without a built-in mental content. Our knowledge and understanding comes from our experiences and perceptions, therefore, we are formed solely by our environment and circumstances.

The purpose for presenting these two opposing theories is not to debate on which is right or wrong, but to establish the foundation on which the subsequent stories and examples are based.

Principles of The Law of Nature

The law of nature is inbuilt in every created thing. It is what sustains every creation and gives order to everything. This law is what sustains balance in nature, and so the tree does not think that it is a giraffe, nor does the mango seed not produce apple fruits. It maintains order.

Through the help of the law of nature, the sun does not confuse itself with the moon, even though they occasionally cross each other thereby causing the solar eclipse; a bird is created to fly, but when it is caged, it cannot express its right to spread its wings

and fly; a fish is destined to swim, but when it is taken out of the water, it dies after a while if it is not returned to its natural habitat
(water on time; trees and plants grow by taking in the carbon dioxide they need for their growth, and releasing oxygen into the air for human survival. Everything has its place and function, including you and I. There are laws and principles built in to creation, and when these are respected, they yield the desired results.

The principles and laws that govern nature are inseparable to creation. I see principles as the conditions by which laws become applicable. Every law has conditions to safe-guard it. A baby is never taught how to grow, yet, it follows certain patterns to attain growth. When a child is not growing as he or she should, the physicians get worried about the normality of this child. I once had to abort a pregnancy at twelve weeks, because the fetus was not following the normal growth pattern, resulting to the chances of survival at less than five percent. It was a painful ordeal, one that we had no choice over, but we had to let go of the pregnancy due to the unfavorable growth conditions of the fetus.

The patterns and sequences from childhood to adulthood are programmed in one's self. A person cannot refuse these principles and laws as this will mean self-destruction. People who refuse to self-improve in order to become who they ought to be, are sabotaging their lives, and depriving the rest of humanity of the great potentials they possess. Like I said, everyone has a role to fulfil on earth, no existence is an accident or useless.

The Tamed Nature

The tamed nature happens when animals are abducted from their natural habitat and trained to have a less violent nature, a custom very well known to us. These animals can never survive in their natural habitat when released, especially if they were too domesticated during their taming process. There are also cases where children are being found and raised by animals, these children are known as feral children. The story of Oxana Malaya of Ukraine is one of the most famous and successful stories of its kind. This woman was said to be perfectly normal at birth. However, due to abuse and neglect by her parents, she ended up living in the family backyard amongst the dogs.

Authorities found her at the age of seven and a half, walking on both hands and limps, behaving like one of the dogs. Oxana underwent several treatments and education to get her back to a "normal" state. The story of Oxana is a successful story because she has been able to get some "normality", though there is a part of her intellect that remains underdeveloped. The rehabilitation of other feral children has not always been successful, just as the rehabilitation of domesticated wild animals has not been successful either. The law of nature is so powerful that when applied correctly, it yields the required result, but sometimes, an aspect of nature can require taming for a specific reason and for a set period. Moreover, taming should always be done in compliance with the law and principles of nature.

The principal duty and purpose of humans on earth is to take care of the earth and all that is in it for nature to yield more positive results and benefits to all. Every talent and or gift is for this purpose.

A passage in the Bible states that, creation waits in eager expectation for the children of God to be revealed. The meaning of this is: for the law of nature to be effective, one needs to Become. Anything done disregarding the principles and law of nature leads to chaos, disorder, and even rebellion. The fish cannot survive outside of its natural habitat. Any attempt to bring the fish out of its habitat without creating that same conducive environment for it leads to its death. A fish confined to a place for too long will likely not survive in its natural habitat when released without proper attention. The difference between human beings and other creatures, is the power of the will. It is the reason why humans are custodians, protectors, and co-creators of nature. We will go deeper into the aspect of the power of the will in Part two, where we will also deal with fear and the paradigm of fear.

OPPORTUNITIES IN CRISIS

During my early days of work, I used to be amazed at the reactions of my co-workers to some setbacks. As I discussed their reactions to the man who was my former coordinator back then, he told me something that has stuck with me ever since that time. He told me that, *"it is in crisis that we discover the true character of a person."*

Whenever there is a crisis, you see different characters being displayed. It is during this period of trouble that you separate the leaders from the followers, the givers from the takers, the quick tempered from the coolheaded, the peacemakers from the troublemakers. Crisis highlights one's true nature.

However, I also found out that when you are not aware of who you are, you adapt to situations due to how you have been trained to respond. Take the example of Oxana, the woman mentioned earlier, as she didn't know about her identity, and as a girl living amongst dogs, her response to crisis was like that of dogs. Later, through education and rehabilitation efforts, she discovered she was more than that. She is a full-grown woman now with rights, feelings, and needs like any other person.

Whenever there is a crisis, you will either approach it positively or negatively depending on the angle you are seeing it. There is a story about a Sower that planted seeds during a drought season. The drought was said to be very severe, yet he had faith he would succeed. He sowed, and as the story goes, he reaped a hundredfold. He was faced with a crisis and could have chosen to either stop planting or to go and look for better pastures elsewhere to plant his seeds. Instead, the Sower acted on faith and faced the crisis head on.

My own experiences have taught me to see crisis as an opportunity. I faced some difficulties even as a young child, but as the old saying goes; *"what does not kill you makes you stronger."*

My departure from Ghana to Belgium, where I currently reside, came with new challenges as well. Firstly, the challenges of living with a man I had not seen for the most of my life, my father. Then the challenges of learning a new language, adapting to a new culture and environment, overcoming racism due to my dark-skin color which before then wasn't an issue to me. And then, the challenge of not having any money for the university, yet holding on and moving towards that goal. One major thing I have learned through every crisis is to be quiet by silencing all other voices and listening to the whisper amid the storm.

Every crisis offers opportunities to those that can see it and use it to their advantage, just like the eagle.

The eagle is a fascinating bird. It is said to be the king of the birds. One fascinating thing about it is that it makes its nest very high on the mountain. This nest is made uncomfortable for the little ones to push them out of their comfort zone and learn to fly. Its babies are taught from the very beginning of their lives to fly or die trying. This type of training might seem hard to some people, but to those who belong to the hunting kingdom, this is the best training to give a young hunter.

I feel I had to go through some tough times just like the baby eagle to learn how to fly and to help others go through this journey of life.

Eagles have a way of using circumstances to their advantage. When the clouds gather, and there is a storm, the eagle finds the eye of the storm and uses the raging storm to lift itself high above the clouds, to where it is peaceful. This allows the eagle to glide and rest its wings. In the meantime, all the other birds hide in the branches and leaves of trees.

I have learnt to look at difficult and challenging issues from a helicopter view, that is, from above. I look at things from a broad way and then narrow them down. This allows me to analyze the underlining problems and helps me to know the choices to make. It might sound unreasonable to some people while in this process, because normally, to get above the storm, one must first go through it and that is not always an easy thing to do. The truth is, however, revealed when you are able to get above the storm to rest and wait for clarity after the storm goes down.

When faced with a challenge, we can do two things: Either face it and use it to our advantage or allow the challenge to overpower us.

Take a minute to check which category you belong to and be honest with yourself because, only through this you can know the steps to take to become you.

3. You are You

"What we know matters, but who we are matters more."

– Brené Brown

As the law of nature clearly defines, everything and everyone has a place and a function to fulfil in life. For instance, an apple tree can never produce orange fruits or pear fruits, so also, a monkey cannot claim to be a human being. A dressed-up monkey remains a monkey. No matter the burdens you are carrying or that may seem to overpower you, you are still you. Just as a butterfly is still a butterfly despite starting its life as a caterpillar, so are you still unique no matter your starting point in life.

The Butterfly

The journey of a butterfly is intriguing. This colorful insect starts its life's journey as a tiny egg. Then a caterpillar is born out of this egg. This caterpillar sheds its skin many times as it grows, then it reaches a stage where it retreats to solitude. It is in this isolation period that the most remarkable transformation takes place; the birth of the full-grown butterfly which is more colorful, graceful and beautiful to the eye than when it was in the caterpillar phase.

The lifespan of this insect is just three to four weeks, but its existence brings joy both to nature and to humans. Imagine if the caterpillar said, *"well, if I transform into this beautiful creature, my life expectancy will reduce, so I will not do it."* What would become of the flowers desperately in need of help for pollination? How would our gardens and parks look like in the spring and summer without these lovely creatures? The caterpillar cannot stop its transformation even if it wants to, due to the law of nature. Only human beings can choose to be or not to be.

You hold the master key to your destiny.

YOU ARE AS STRONG AS YOUR CHARACTER

During crisis period, our characters are spotlighted as if they are being held under observation in a mental facility. In my native language, which is Twi, we have an expression that a character is like a pregnancy, no matter how hard you try to hide it, it must show up one day. Also, a crisis period allows our characters to be polished. While growing up, I often wondered why some people were so mean. Was it something they developed or was it just how they were? It took me years to come to this very realization: We are who we choose to be despite the circumstances. Some people are mean because they choose to be mean.

Agreeably, we do not always have the choice of what or how we are educated and how we socialize, and this impacts our character as well. I wrote one of my thesis on the phenomena of child soldiers, namely *"The child soldiers in the Lord Resistance Army (LRA) in Northern Uganda."* Most of the children were kidnapped by the raging soldiers and forced to do unspeakable things. The process of rehabilitating the children that have been rescued and or able to escape back into the society was and still is challenging. The question I kept asking myself as I wrote the thesis was *"Will the integration of these children into the society be successful?"* The additional problem with the LRA is also that, large number of children are born in captivity. These children know nothing else than what they experience and witness. Can they ever live a "normal" life, or is all hope lost for them? Is there something in them that can be salvaged, as Rousseau believed? Can re-education bring them to self-realization? Or is hope lost for them if all they know and have is what they have experienced?

Undoubtedly, these are challenges faced by the society and the individuals. One may ask, Is society not the originator of this dilemma in the first place? Well, societies consist of individuals and when these individuals are broken, the society is also broken. One cannot and should not be seen separately from the other.

CULTURAL, TRADITIONAL AND RELIGIOUS BARRIERS

In accordance with the African tradition, I have learned to have great respect for the elderly. That includes not talking when the elderly people are talking. Growing up, I was always reminded of the consequences of being too curious, which was and is still considered as disrespectful. I was sometimes inquisitive, always trying to understand what the adults were talking about and tried to ask some questions. But, according to tradition, children should not interfere in adults' conversations. Another act that could easily put me into trouble was when I dared to give something to someone with my left hand. That was a forbidden act! I was constantly on the look-out to make sure I did not breach any traditional rules. Now, as a mother, I see myself doing the same with my children, teaching them not to be too curious around adults and to have respect for them. Teaching them also to give things with their right hands to other people. When they ask me why, like children do, I simply say *"because that is how it should be done or because it is more respectful."*

This is not a reasonable explanation to me, but this is what I have been trained to believe and so I pass it on to my children.

There are some cultural habits transferred and applied without question. Cultures and traditions are regarded as untouchable and unquestionable, while the whole fabric of creation, including humans, is subjected to change. If change is inevitable in our daily lives, shouldn't we be able to question some man-made rules and customs?

The same with religion. In religion, people are conditioned into submission. Submission is interpreted as accepting whatever you get in life. Religion puts fear in the hearts of people and takes away their power of choice. It can be summarized as the acts or rituals performed and lived by in respect to a deity, and it originates mostly and is sustained by the emotion called fear. Religion is the opposite of faith, because faith is founded on the emotion called love. We will go deeper into these emotions in the next Part.

In as much as some cultural, religious and traditional rules give guidelines and moral values, they can also be overbearing and overly abused. To Become, one must look beyond these barriers and break through them. Take the best of the barriers and make your own culture along the way. As you Become, it is the culture you create that makes you.

The question of who you are is a question that only you can answer. To answer it correctly, you must be willing to search deep into your soul and remove layers of masks covering the treasures buried under. There is no doubt a correlation between nature and nurture. We are born as individuals with our talents, unique characters, and attributes. However, these are shaped and influenced by the environment we find ourselves in. This environment can enhance our development or hinder us, and ultimately change our naturally in-built attributes and talents.

What have you experienced or presently going through that seems to swallow you up or make you feel there is no way out? You can find the keys to unlock the seemingly closed doors if you are willing to submit yourself to the process. No other person can do this for you except to give you a shoulder to lean on.

Only you can answer the question of who you are and choose not to give up. Are you, however, prepared to do this and to take the necessary steps to achieve this?

PART TWO: BODY OF EMOTIONS

Humans cannot function without emotions. Without emotions, we become robotic, apathetic, and detached. Emotions play a significant role in our existence. Due to the different kinds of emotions our minds and bodies produce, we survive every situation, communicate our feelings, and build our realities through and by them. Thus, emotions are very influential, powerful and can either block or enhance the hidden potentials buried under the layers of masks.

Because of my experiences, I was a body full of emotions. One minute I would be genuinely happy and the other I would be sad or angry, like I explained in Part one. I learned somehow to conceal my feelings and that was my way of surviving.

This section of this book deals with the effects, the importance, and the role of emotions in decision-making. We will study the purpose of emotions and the importance of controlled emotions. We will also understand the mechanism behind certain emotions and their origins.

4. Effects of Emotions

"You can tell the greatness of a man by what makes him angry."

- Abraham Lincoln

Like I said earlier, we are wired with emotions. The body and the mind work together to produce the kind of emotions suitable for a situation. Emotions are for various reasons; the principal one is for survival. When an experience is registered in the mind as painful, the brain will trigger painful emotions in similar situations, warning the body and the soul to be aware of such experience. We tend to avoid painful, sorrowful, or negative emotions and seek after the feel-good emotions. That was my survival hack. I avoided the sorrowful and painful emotions by creating a different reality where everything was good, where I was loved, cared for, and protected against threats. This reality was my escape paradise. Whenever I felt threatened, I created the feel-good reality and I was always in it. The world around me did not seem to bother me that much whenever I was in my feel-good reality. It was like being in two places at the same time, that is, my physical body would be present in a place, but my spirit and soul would be in a different place. I would be seeing what was happening to me, but not feel the pain that much, not that it didn't hurt, but my mind would not be there, thus numbing the pain or whatever negative emotions I was supposed to feel at that time. To outsiders I had no problem, I seemed happy and, also did well in school. Little did they know that I had so concealed my real feelings until the reality seemed like a dream.

As I grew older, I began to search for some truths within me. I embarked on understanding the role of emotions in my life. I realized that, running away from my reality by exchanging one emotion for the other did not change the situation nor make anything better. This is the reason some people become addicted to the feel-good emotion and always want to be there, because the alternative is too painful to bear. It is what pushes some people into drugs, alcohol, and all manner of addictions. It is futile to attempt escaping reality because it never works, at least not in the long term. It simply prolongs people's experiences and derails them from their journey of becoming who they ought to be.

CATEGORIES OF EMOTIONS

From my experience, I began to distinguish three major categories of emotions on which my feelings were built. They are: Love, Hate, and Fear. I realized that the positive feelings I experienced in my created world and transferred to reality were from a deep craving for love. Due to what I suffered, hate was always lurking at the door in the form of anger and self-hatred, and out of fear of rejection, I would comply with situations that I did not like or were not favorable to me. Fear has played such a dubious role in my life, a role that I will go deeper into in Chapter 6 of this book.

In my opinion, these three categories of emotions regulated my life. I have listed and categorized below some of the emotions I felt had a very strong impact on me. These are not the only emotions I experienced or that exist, because emotions are very complex and never occur as a singular factor. I am not an expert on the issue of emotions, so these categories are based on my own experiences and how I have come to identify emotions and their effects on me.

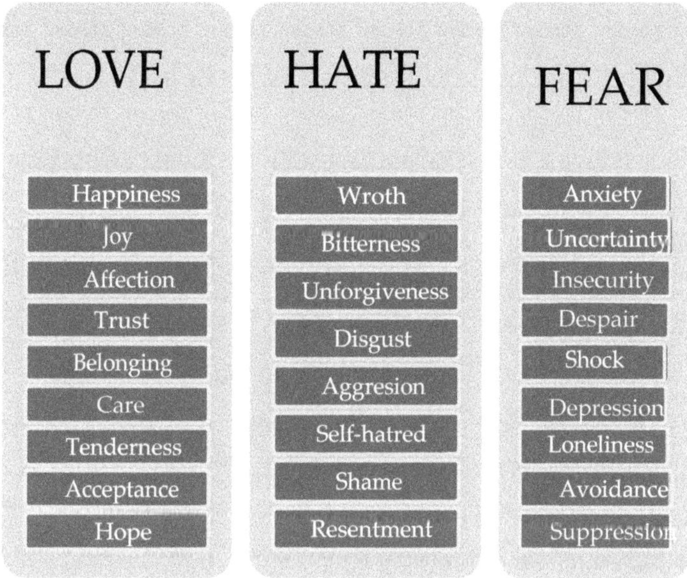

Love, Hate, and Fear are very different. As different as they are, I noticed these categories share some common emotions. What I mean to say, is that you can find these emotions in all of these categories, with such emotions being inspiration, ambition, desire, passion, disappointment and so on. Again, I must say that this is not based on any scientific research, but based on my own observations. Now, let us take a closer look at these categories by taking passion for an example. Passion is a powerful emotion that can come from a place of love, but

also, from a place of hate and fear. Out of love for self, some people begin to do work-outs passionately for a better body shape or to be in good health. This same passion for work-outs can come from hatred for body fat or can start from fear of being rejected by a group or society. It is also true for inspiration, desire, ambition, and so on.

There was an incident that happened during my stay in my uncle's house, it was on my 8th birthday. Like every other birthday, my mother made sure I celebrated it because I always insisted on celebrating my birthday, so she always made that day special no matter where I was. She would bake a very beautiful cake, buy some soft-drinks and make a special meal for me on that day. So, on this fateful day, she came to visit me at my uncle's house with a cake and some drinks, to celebrate my 8th birthday. But as fate would have it, she found me in a very bad condition. I had a wound on my left leg inflicted on me by the eldest son of my uncle. This wound had been infected due to lack of proper care. She was heart-broken when she saw this and for the first time, I saw anger and unbelief in her eyes, and at the same time, I felt this warmth of care and love. Instead of celebrating,

she lashed out at my uncle and aunty for their lack of care. My aunty tried to talk her way out with all kinds of lies, but I was still mesmerized by what I had witnessed in my mother. I thought that surely, she would take me home with her. But after everything, I was surprised that she left me behind, in my uncle's house and for the very first time in my life, I had a public break-down. I threw myself to the ground, screaming, kicking, and begging to be taken home. I was filled with horror, despair, unbelief, anger and hate in the form of bitterness. When all that I did, did not make any difference, those feelings turned to apathy. Apathy was a neutral state for me, a place where everything and nothing mattered, it became my new comfort-zone.

I didn't care about what would happen to me anymore, or what was going on around me. I felt so disappointed but I didn't know who I was disappointed at, was it at myself, my mother, my hosts, my surroundings? Again, I withdrew to my safe zone of apathy, I escaped to my created world that I did not even feel the pains from the punishment my hosts inflicted on me for the humiliation they suffered from my mother and my tantrums.

YOUR EMOTIONS, YOUR CHARACTER

Emotions regulate our behaviors and shape our characters. I behaved as expected of me. As an only child, I tried not to disappoint my mother, so I always had a bold and happy face when I was with people. I tried to hold back the inquisitive part of me and to put up the emotion suitable for the occasion at any given time. I realized also I had a strong will, meaning that I knew mostly what I wanted and what I needed, but out of fear of punishment and the need to respect traditions, I had to suppress it. At times it felt like being a chameleon, changing colors, so as not to let the people around me down or not to let them see the real me. I preferred to be invisible to avoid hurts, insults, or being preyed on. In public, however, I did put up an appearance as required. The times where I could be myself were, when I was playing with my friends, in Sunday School classes, and or dancing. I also loved acting in dramas, because I could hide behind the masks to convey my true feelings while different roles.

Each of these categories has its own characteristics. To me, Hate for self and Fear were more prominent than Love. Hate came, amongst others, in the form of bitterness, anger, torment, low self-esteem, and unforgiveness. While Fear was there to constantly remind me of my mistakes, both the present ones and those yet to come. It reminded me that no matter what I did or thought to do, it would never be enough and that I would be nothing. Fear was my daily companion; it was the leading emotion among the three. Love seemed unreachable, like a dream to pursue. The thought of it sounded and felt good only in my imaginations.

I had to go through a process of self-awareness to identify the different emotions I experienced, what triggered them, and the role each of them played in my life. I thought that I did not deserve to be loved, because who would love a broken vessel like me? I also thought I was incapable of loving others. To experience a complete change in my life, I had to make conscious and careful analysis of my emotions and intensify my prayers as I became more aware of their effects in my life.

The first and most important step I took was learning to LOVE myself. It meant accepting myself not as I was, but as what I can become. This meant, learning to look at myself in the mirror and see beyond the visible, see the hidden treasures waiting patiently to be revealed and embodied. This required and still does require, a deliberate and conscious attitude toward my use of time in front of the mirror. It is easy to look and not see anything because of the pain and lies that present themselves first, but it takes courage to wade through them to discover yourself.

The second step was learning to FORGIVE myself. This part seemed and is still the hardest thing to do: FORGIVENESS of ONE'S SELF. I found out that it is easier for us to forgive others but in most cases, it is hard to forgive ourselves and that is why we avoid the act of self-reflection. Each time something would go wrong, or if I had a disagreement with someone, I would quickly take the blame just to allow peace to reign, overly willing to forgive the other, but then hold back grudges against myself. I would ask myself, *"why didn't I protect myself enough, why did I allow things to go that fare, why did I not talk and face whatever the consequences might have been? And so on."*

Instead, I would take the blame and feed the Fear and Hate emotions with these thoughts.

The third step is a continual step of SELF-IMPROVEMENT. Like the caterpillar, I had to retreat and do an intense self-evaluation, pulling off the mask layer by layer to find the triggers of each emotion and why it was triggered. It was then the reality of things began to dawn on me. I realized that I am more than my emotions therefore I cannot allow them to control me. The journey has not been easy, it is still an ongoing one, because the process of becoming never ends. Nevertheless, the process was and still is necessary. There is a saying that goes as follows, *"You cannot give what you don't have."* That is very true because it is only what you have that you can give and what you give determines the quality of what you receive.

Take a minute and reflect on yourself. Can you identify the emotions that are controlling you, and where they are coming from? How are they affecting your daily life and the people around you?

Take your time to do this and do it well, because it is essential in the process for you to Become.

EMOTIONS AND DECISION-MAKING

Our emotions affect our actions, thoughts, mood, and therefore our decision-making. Have you heard of the saying, "follow your heart?" It is the most deceptive statement we can make and or advice. Why do I say so? Physically, the heart is an organ formed out of muscles. It keeps us alive by pumping blood to all the organs in our body. The heart, thus, plays a vital role which is; without the heart, we die. The heart, however, does not have any decision-making abilities. So, what does this saying mean?

We have what I have come to understand and classified as two non-physical 'hearts' namely, the mind and the inner-man (our subconscious state. The reason I said that the statement is deceitful is because, we are never told which of the hearts to follow, so we are not conscious of their effects on us. A decision taken from the subconscious is entirely different from that of the mind. Though both represent the heart, a decision made from the mind can easily be overturned. Many times, we use these words 'have changed my mind' to identify a decision made from the mind. On the other hand, a decision made from the subconscious mind is more difficult to change because it does not come easily. It takes consciousness and intentionality to take a decision from the subconscious mind.

It can be dangerous and deceiving to follow your heart without knowing which of the hearts you are following.

THE IMPORTANCE OF CONTROLLED EMOTIONS

Some people allow their emotions to greatly influence everything about them, and that can be very dangerous. I realized that there was one thing I could control, it was the ability to withdraw and analyze my decisions before taking any step further.

It doesn't mean emotions shouldn't be present when deciding on some issues, but it shouldn't be the most overpowering force. Decisions influenced by Love, Fear, or Hate, have different consequences and can end-up well or badly. Every decision has consequences, but when we can control our emotions, we can put things into perspective before taking certain steps, so that in the process, we would have to think about the consequences and how to deal with them.

Deciding from a place of Hate, Fear or Love as a singular component, is the most dangerous thing to do. These categories of emotions overcloud every logical reasoning.

Before making any serious decision, it is necessary to analyze where the thought is coming from, why you are taking that step or decision, and where it might lead you. I know we cannot do this in every situation, that is why I said it is necessary mostly when it is an important decision where the notion of following your heart is involved or could be involved.

Everyone can master their emotions. It is a matter of choice, a topic we will go deeper into in the next chapter.

5. The Power of Will

"Strength does not come from physical capacity. It comes from an indomitable will."

– Mahatma Gandhi

WILL is a complex issue and even more so when it has to do with relationships, including the relationship with one's self, but most of us don't think about it this way. The most precious and the most misunderstood gift the Creator gave us is the WILL. I believe, despite everything I have been through, that we are created by a loving and merciful

God, who, out of His love for us, gave us a free mind, which is called the WILL. The greatest Architect of all time designed us as free beings, not bound by anything but by our own choices.

That is why we are co-creators of His project just like a builder is a co-creator of a building project with any architect. This is what differentiates us from other creatures. As I wrote earlier on, certain choices, cultures, traditions, and religious beliefs limit us from reaching our full potentials. The purpose of the will is to free us and not to enslave us, it is also to lead us in becoming who we have already been made to be. We can only become who we are meant to be if we develop a healthy relationship with ourselves and with the Creator.

TRUE FREEDOM

The will, on its own, can be self-centered and very destructive. It comes in the form of pride, greed, deception, arrogance, ignorance, and so on. When the will is used wrongly due to ignorance, it dominates, controls, manipulates and takes over the person. The purpose was never to make selfish people out of us who dominate over other people, but to willingly humble ourselves for the benefit of all. The will is also meant to set us free, yet in its natural form, it enslaves us, this is a paradox!

The world will be in chaos if we always want to have our way all the time. History has shown that most wars and most sociological problems people experience are the results of the persistence and selfish enforcement of the WILL. The only way to be free is to be willing to give up a part of this will and align it with that of others.

As a teacher, I like to engage my students when teaching them, by challenging them to question some things. I taught the subject of freedom in different classes. I asked them to define what freedom meant to them. After each session, the general conclusion on freedom was the following:

Freedom is the right to exercise your will without fear of persecution, slavery, and all forms of exclusion.

I went further on to present some scenarios to them based on their definition. One of such scenarios was:

What would you do if you had a neighbor that plays loud music till very late in the night every day, and when you complained about it, he said that he was exercising his right?

It was interesting to see the reactions of the students towards these scenarios. After much deliberations, they agreed that everyone has the right to freedom and must be assured and secured about it. However, how to make sure that this right doesn't make another person suffer is not always clear. That is why we look up to an external force like the Law to help in regulating this, and that leads me to the following question:

If an external force is needed to secure the freedom of all, is this then not a limiting factor of this same freedom?

At the end, all the students concluded that freedom should not be at the expense of the other. If everyone is willing to give up a bit of their freedom for the sake of a peaceful co-existence with the other person, then everyone can be truly free.

As a young girl, I loved writing, but I was limited in the things I wrote due to the high level of monitoring and lack of privacy I found myself in. I loved keeping a diary, so one day, I wrote in my very empty diary the following:

I wish I was free, free like a bird. When will these chains of bondage be broken for me to be free, for me to breathe again? I feel tired. I don't have the strength to fight anymore, I can't. I want to be free.

My father concluded after reading it that I wanted to run away from home. Every attempt to explain myself got me into more trouble. The freedom I was talking about was different from what my students and my father defined. I was talking about mental, spiritual, and emotional freedom. When the topic of freedom is being discussed, these three aspects of freedom are largely neglected but they are the most vital part of freedom. Though my students were right in their definition of freedom, their definition was not complete. True freedom is above all circumstances, that is why someone can be in prison and yet feel free. Equally, one can be free physically and yet be in bondage mentally.

In relationships, we must let go of things that are not beneficial for our existence. This is give and take. The bond created in us when we accept who we are is also like that. The will of the mind has to align with that of the inner self to become one. There is an inner struggle when this is not the case.

Alienation with one's self is when you feel completely lost, not knowing, or recalling who you are. You make decisions based on the will and wants of others and not based on who you are.

It is equally important to control our emotions by taming our will. If we always have our way in every situation, we act foolishly and there is no wisdom in it. Taming is different from being caged. Taming is befriending our will, knowing it, being one with it and knowing how and when to use it. Being caged, on the other hand, is the absence of freedom in all ramifications. It is when you have no control over your choices coupled with when your choices are not your own.

You must be able to control your emotions because by doing so you will be able to control your power. This ability is called meekness. Meekness is the willingness to control your emotions and tame your will. It takes a lot of strength and courage to constraint something as powerful as the will. While some people may see this as a weakness, it is strength personified. Meekness is constraining your ability to exercise your power. It is when you have the right to react in a certain way, but decide not to. For example, you have the right to take revenge on a certain evil act done against you, but choose not to do that, but rather, you choose to forgive. That is wisdom applied. Meekness is not submissiveness or foolishness, as some might think it to be, it is where the real power is, and in Abraham Lincoln's words,

"It is better to remain silent and be thought a fool than to speak out and remove all doubt."

In the process to become, and to be truly free, it is essential to know the will, understand its role, and know how to use it.

Circumstances and difficulties of life can make it hard to pause and think over events. Most of the time, it seems like we don't have a choice over certain situations, but the truth remains that life is all about choices. We will understand this better as we read further below.

CHOICE IS NOT AN OPTION

Some people think that making a choice is an option. Yes, you can choose out of different options, but a choice itself

is not an option, it is an obligation. When you encounter some circumstances, most times, you have two options; to act or not to act, to move or to stay, to live or to die. In the story of the Sower, he chooses to stay in a place of drought and sow despite the odds against him. It was a choice. He could have decided to leave that place, but instead, he chooses to stay. When we encounter a crisis, our survival instinct sets in. We either face it head-on or we lay low, wait, and hope it passes away soon. There is never a thing as "no choice" as some may think, because we are faced daily with choices. These choices are primary influenced by our emotional state at that moment.

The power in the gift of the will is that we can determine our fate by the choices we make. To some people, this is liberation, while to others, it is a dilemma. This means that we are responsible for the choices we make. We are both the architect and the builder of our lives. When we make a mistake, it is our fault an not that of others. So, to avoid this load

of responsibilities, we often prefer to put the 'choice' and by extension, the will, away from ourselves, because it is easier to blame other people for our misfortunes or mistakes. People are blamed for the bad economy, for the lack of progress and for being at the same spot for many years. However, we don't have to dwell in our past and blame it for our current situation. I did not choose most of the things that happened to me in the past, but I am conscious that I can change my future by the choices I make today. You can also decide to make good choices and change your future.

Earlier on in this book, I wrote that we are all destined for something. Some people may interpret it to mean that, no matter what they do or where they are, they will always be what they are meant to be. Well, I disagree with this because what we will be can only happen if we take the right steps and stay on the path that leads to our destination. An athlete that decides not to put in the necessary work to be the best will not be the best. Likewise, a builder who does not commit systematically and methodically to a building project, respecting all the regulations and recommendations of the architect, will fail miserably. It takes commitment, hard work, determination, responsibility, motivation, and diligence, amongst others, to fulfill destiny. That is why I said that the will is the most complex and often a misunderstood component in our existence.

RIGHT IS NOT GOOD

Every created thing has an inherent understanding of what is right and what is wrong. Right is different from good. Good is determined by what culture, tradition, religion, rules and the law define it to be and therefore acceptable. This type of definition of good can change anytime depending on the group, social status and other criteria. A popular group can define good based on the values and norms they uphold. An armed robber is bad by the law but is good to his own group. Even the law made by men is not entirely free from bias because traditions, religion and beliefs have great impact on these laws, but Right is more than that. Right is universal, above all and everyone. It is also non-negotiable.

Most of the time, good is called right due to the lack of understanding of them. We all do this, we make decisions based on what feels good to us and call it right, being ignorant of the fact that these two are not the same. A murder is regarded as wrong in every culture and or religion. However, it becomes acceptable or judged differently based on the conditions surrounding the murder and the criteria on which the judgement was made. So even though murder is not right, two people convicted for it may not receive the same sentence. This is because the judgement is based on the notion of good and not based on the notion of right, so the act of murder itself is not tried. A person who commits mass killing and is found to have been ideologically inspired, is considered a terrorist for one group and a freedom fighter or martyr for another group, depending on the angle we look at it. The very act of shedding human blood, which by all is considered wrong, is not really the focus here, but rather, it is the motives that led to the killing that are judged.

As young as I was, I knew that what I was going through was wrong, I knew, from the depth of my soul, that what that man was doing to me was wrong. That was why I felt so sick, dirty and ashamed each time, but the unwritten rules of engagement made me feel that I was not supposed to talk about it and gave me the impression to just accept it.

Depending on which group we belong to or feel affiliated with, we will make choices based on the rules of engagement that is considered good and acceptable. We make decisions based on what makes us feel good and call it right, so the next time you are faced with a choice, please, take the time to evaluate if it is good or right by asking yourself some questions like: Why and from where am I making this decision? Is it based on a universal truth or is it based on what is perceived to be acceptable and regarded as the norm in the society I find myself?

There was a time I was faced with a fundamental choice. It happened some years ago, when I met my boyfriend who is now my husband, and wanted to introduce him to my parents. My parents refused to meet him just because he is from a different country. My husband is a Nigerian from the Igbo tribe, and that alone was enough reason for my father not to give him a chance of acquaintance. To my parents, they were trying to protect me from the unknown, therefore they considered their action as good. To me, it was not right. No one chooses the family, ethnicity, or country he or she is born into, so why should it be a criterion to judge someone? Today, many people are facing this level of discrimination on a daily basis.

Judging someone based on their ethnicity, religion and or country is not right and also unacceptable. My parents did not consider if their decision was right, but since they considered it as good, they expected that I obeyed them. I had the choice to accept their decision as good by reasoning with them, but then I would be untrue to myself.

However, I choose the path of right irrespective of the outcome of the relationship in the future. There comes a time you must stand for what is right no matter the cost, because it is only by standing for what is right that you can truly Become.

When you choose to stand for what is RIGHT, most times, you may find yourself standing alone. The path of RIGHT is very lonely, and often misunderstood, and only the bold and courageous dare to walk through it. Examine your choices, compare if they are right or good, and know what ideologies, rules, laws, or in other words, what philosophies are influencing you in one way or the other.

CONSEQUENCES OF WRONG USE OF WILL

The problem with the will is that, although it is to free us, we can only be truly free if we are all willing to give up a bit of our will for the benefit of others. Like I wrote earlier, it is a give and take situation. If you are someone who only takes from others, then you are considered a cheat, selfish and self-seeking. If you are someone who only gives to others, you will never be fulfilled because you will always feel used, abused, and neglected. That is also a form of self-seeking. The purpose of the will is to complete each other by completing ourselves first. Your Becoming is essential for the people around you as much as it is essential for you.

In today's society, it is all about oneself, that is: me, myself, and I. An individual is encouraged to enforce his or her will regardless of the price society will pay for the it. I see a trend amongst the youth as I interact with them, the trend of putting their will and wants above every other thing. This indeed has been the case for youths in general across all generation, however, with the current generation, it has gone to a different level. Most youths find voluntary work to be burdensome and a waste of time. When they are asked why they don't to volunteer, the reply I get most of the time is *"why should we do that for free?"* There must be a reward in exchange for their time and this reward is mostly expressed in monetary value. This attitude makes them forget that there are other benefits that come from the act of selfless servitude, which in most cases, are much more valuable. Every knowledge gained and or connection made can be the bridge that will take one to the next level in life. In this journey, nothing should be taking for granted and that is unfortunately what the youth of nowadays do.

This is a wrong use of the will. It produces selfish and self-seeking people who have little or no connection with their environment, and because no man is an island, this becomes an obstacle for the progress of both the society and the individual.

The will must work together with the law of nature and spiritual law to yield the best result. As written in the Bible, *"For creation waits in eager expectation for the children of God to be revealed..."*, man must be willing to take up his responsibility by taking charge of the process of controlling his will in order for nature to give the best result. When we ignore this and enforce our will, we get disorder within us and within society.

6.The Paradigm of Fear

"May your choices reflect your hopes, not your fears."

- Nelson Mandela

Fear was my constant companion, as stated earlier in the three categories of emotions. It had this awful and at the same time, controlling effect on me. One minute it crippled and paralyzed me that I couldn't speak or move. Then the next minute, it was pushing me to do something to stay alive, not to accept the status quo.

Fear is dubious in every way. One of the ways it is defined is through its acronym, namely, "FALSE EVIDENCE APPEARING REAL." This definition is very accurate but does not express the totality of the fear I came to know. I have come to know fear, or better still, the reactions to fear in different ways. Fear is to warn us of emerging or prominent danger. It is the awareness of the presence of something that could either harm us and or the people around us. The response to this emotion, however, can be different.

In this chapter, I will introduce some of the different types of fear to you. It might help you identify which kind of fear you are more likely allowing to influence you.

PARALYZING FEAR

Fear in its natural form is not a monster we should be afraid of. It is an emotion to warn us of danger in all its forms. However, the response to this emotion can make a monster out of it, making it become false evidence appearing real. Fear has many forms of expression such as: desperation, uncertainty, insecurity, danger, anxiety, panic, frustration, worry, and procrastination. Out of fear for the unknown, some people can choose to remain in a harmful and even destructive environment, while some can develop hate for a group of people, which is called phobia. It is unfortunate how some people allow the fear of the unknown to influence them. The product of this type of fear allows prejudice and discrimination to fill their hearts and lead to blind hatred.

For many years, I lived with the monster called fear. Though it was not visible to the outside world, yet it was so alive within me. Fear made me lose my voice, hate myself, and lose all hope. In my dreams, it was there. While awake, it constantly reminded me of what I could never be. I projected this fear in every situation around me and reacted to its effects. To cover up this crippling fear, I developed the habit of laughing over situations or masking my fear with an *'I don't care attitude (apathy)'*, but at the same time, I was terrified inside of me. I could see myself crying out for help, yet the cry was muffled, never voiced out, or only heard when I was alone. This type of fear is the type that paralyzes your very being.

As a child, I bed-wetted almost every night. Sometimes, I would wake up in wet clothes even after waking up more than ten times in the night. I was ashamed of it, especially when I was living with my uncle. While living in his house, I was given torn old clothes to use as my sleeping mat, as that was what my aunty thought I deserved due to my condition. On one occasion, I was wrapped in all my wet clothes and sleeping rags and forced to walk through the streets. The children in the neighborhood bullied me as I walked through the streets of the barrack. As shameful as it was, coupled with the daily beatings I received, it never stopped the monsters of fear and hate from coming out in the night. At night, I was afraid to fall asleep because I saw these monsters in different forms, both humans and beasts, everywhere around me. I also got very angry with myself. I thought and believed that I was the cause of all that was happening to me, and I was angry about why I couldn't just stop it. Hate and fear worked hand in hand, each took a role after the other.

To live above the shame and pain, I started building up some tricks. Before anyone commented on anything, I would be the first to comment on it or call it out and laugh over it, thus taking away the effect of the power of fear and shame from me. For example, the issue of bedwetting. I started to joke about it, making funny remarks, that after a while, I was left alone. I finally got control over the fear and shame after confronting one of the main attributes of this problem, the cruelest monster of them all, the pedophile event. Nevertheless, the inner struggle continued.

FEAR OF FAILURE

Fear also had another type of power over me. This type of fear made me scale through and not to give up. The thought of it alone scared me and made me more determined to move on. This fear was the fear of failure. Because of it, I preferred to endure the pains while I worked my way forward. The alternative was too costly for me to consider. I had experienced so much negativity around me that failing should have been a natural outcome, but that was something I was determined not to allow. This fear restrained me from keeping certain circles of friends while growing up and helped to keep me focused. I couldn't control what others did or

thought of me, but I could control what became of me.

I believe the fear of failure is inbuilt, a natural survival instinct. It can work as a catalyst to push you forward, and it can also paralyze you. Some people don't try anything at all out of the fear of failure. They rather stay in one place out of this fear. To them, is better not to try at all than to try and fail. There is a proverb that says, *"the devil you know is better than the angel you don't know."* Others stay in a toxic environment out of fear of the unknown, out of uncertainty, and out of insecurity. Many people also don't want to take chances because of the fear of success because they might lose control in the process. Uncertainty for some people is a big mountain to overcome. You can only get what you prepare yourself to get and what you prepare yourself to handle.

The paradigm of fear is that the reaction to it can be a paralyzing force or a motivating force to move you in a certain direction. Fear can challenge you to come out of your comfort zone. For example, when someone is afraid for his life, it can push him to do anything to survive. Yet, this same situation or feeling can paralyze another person from trying anything if the alternative is considered worse than the current situation.

PART THREE: PROCESS TO BECOME

In parts one and two, I showed us some stages to get us prepared for this final stage. The first stage is: *Identifying who you are by peeling off the layers of mask you might be wearing or in a nutshell, just becoming more aware of who you are*. I used my own experiences to explain this process.

The second stage is: *Becoming aware of the emotions that control you and their origins*. The way we perceive things and people, and react to them is rooted in the experiences that we have consciously and or unconsciously absorbed, and yet, they control us through our emotions. As powerful as emotions are, they must be tamed and used wisely in the right circumstance or situation, especially when it comes to decision-making.

In this final part, we will look at the additional requirements needed in the process to become the awesome person we already are. We have hidden treasures in us that can only be fully developed, improved and actualized when we are fully aware of them, nourish them and serve them to others. To do this, firstly, we need to have an idea of who we are, what we possess, and the purpose for which we have them.

Secondly, we need to know how to use what we possess to be effective and fulfilled in life.

7. Own Your Vision

"A man may die nations may rise and fall but an idea lives on. Ideas have endurance without death."

- John F.Kennedy

One day I was asked a question that kept me thinking for a long time. The question was: *"What is your motto in life?"* This question came as a joke. We were a group of friends having fun, and this question came up suddenly. At first, I had to think very well before attempting to answer it. At that moment, we all said whatever came into our minds, however, I kept pondering on the question;

"what is my motto in life?" There seemed to be no answer good enough to the question at that time.

Until then, I thought I had it all figured out: Do good, avoid evil, be at peace with everyone and make the best out of life. I had not yet developed any motto to live by, except what I just listed above, which was not that bad. All I knew was that I was hungry for a change and went about it the best way I could. Until this question, I had not clarified any idea as the motto of my life. After much internal search, I wrote down the following as my motto:

I let go of the past I cannot change, I embrace the present, which is a gift from God, and hold on to the promises of tomorrow. I am endowed with unlimited potential, and I am a gift to my generation.

VISION IS FAITH

I came to realize the grip the past still had on me in the form of fear and hate. It was what motivated me to write down those words. For me to be able to move forward, I must willingly let go of the past. The grip of the past was hindering me from seeing my future. It was influencing my present in the form of mediocrity, fear, and low self-esteem.

I knew I was living below my potentials. I had to see the present as a gift, so that I can correct the wrongs of the past, an opportunity to try again and make new choices that will make my future better. Although the future is yet unknown, one thing is for sure: The choices of today determines tomorrow, and at the same time, tomorrow holds promises of a better today.

Vision is crucial in life. Without vision, anything is tolerated, whereas there is no such thing as anything. Vision gives clarity. I was confused when my vision was not clear. I lived a casual life, as mentioned in earlier passages. All I knew was that, because of fear, I didn't want to fail in life. I didn't want to disappoint my mother as her only child. That was my motivation then, which fell short by all standards. At a point, this reason was no longer enough and satisfying. The biggest mistake to make is to build your vision around people and on emotions. People can disappoint and emotions are unstable.

Vision is seeing a thing before the actual realization of it. It is like faith. Faith is defined in the Bible as the confidence in what we hope for and the assurance about what we do not see. Faith, therefore, is believing in that which is unseen in the visible realm but seen in the invisible realm. It is like a dream that becomes more real when written down. It is necessary that you write down your vision. However, before you can write a vision down, you must first conceive it in your subconscious mind and then, in your mind as a thought or an idea.

Before a building is built, it is first envisioned by an architect, who tries to reproduce every part of the vision on paper. So once a vision is written down, it becomes visible and tangible for all to see. That is why, before a building is built, the technical design of it on paper by the architect gives it life and hope.

Vision therefore is the hope that drives away all fears and (or) gives meaning to life. Vision, therefore, goes together with faith. When you have a vision, you see the roadmap to your future, a glimpse of the possibilities you have. You start to believe in the impossible and work towards the accomplishment of it. Without a clear vision, some walk and live life anyhow, like one with no root or like a wanderer with no destination. They move and live in the direction the wind may blow. While some play the safe game and remain at one spot. This is not a sustainable state to live in.

Vision is the foundation on which a person can shape his or her life. Like a building, if the foundation is not strong enough, the building stands a chance of collapsing. The foundation is laid according to the weight it must carry. Your vision must be as strong as the dreams you are birthing now and in the future. When a vision has no strong foundation, it will not stand the test of time. Visions outlive people, it never dies, and it is judged by generations to come.

Traditions, which produce cultures, are generally seen as visions. However, most traditions are bound to time, thereby, limiting the people and the society to that time. As a foundation, traditions must be strong enough to carry future buildings without too many alterations. When the foundation undergoes too many changes, it can cause a loss of identity, a shaky and unstable ground.

To Become, you must have a strong vision. A vision that will outlive you and is strong enough to carry all your dreams and aspirations. That vision needs time to

develop and grow. So, give it the time it needs to be fully developed and gets refined as you mature with it. It is a foundation on which

you build a strong character and a future. Consequently, it should not undergo drastic changes, however, occasionally, it is necessary to evaluate and upgrade it to the present time. This is one of the reasons it is vital to have a vision that transcends your current time, that spans into the future.

Take your time and go through your vision if you have one. Can it stand the test of time? If you don't have one, then please, write one now. Build a strong foundation for your life, the root out of which many dreams may spring out. To quote the words of Napoleon Hill, *"A man can create nothing which he does not first conceive in the form of an impulse of thought."*

PURPOSE OF VISION

As I began to meditate on the words of my vision, my attitude changed. I began to see beyond what my eyes could see. The promises of the future made me believe more in myself and helped me to push beyond my abilities at that time. Therefore, I added the phrase *'endowed with unlimited potentials'* to my vision, to continually remind me to think and see beyond the ordinary. Seeing myself as a gift, a vessel filled with hidden potentials helped to mold my character. I realized this is what vision does. It guides you, gives you direction and makes you conscious of time. It helps to make you steadfast in life, and like the eagle, the forward direction becomes clear. An eagle sees its prey from a far distance, locks it in its sight, and then, dives from its position towards this prey. The eagle never loses focus but heads straight on for its target. The result is that the eagle is always very successful in most of its hunts.

As the vision started to become a part of my very being, I became more focused, intentional, and committed in life. Where I used to do things anyhow, I began to do them with more conviction, determination and with a goal. As the vision became clearer, it helped me to identify my gifts that were necessary to achieve my purpose. We will go deeper into this topic in the next chapter.

When your direction is clear, you will know which roads to avoid, the people to keep away from and those to keep as friends.

Another characteristic of vision is that it helps to develop your values. In my opinion, values are the preferences you uphold, the principles by which you measure all things. These preferences are translated into ways of acting and thereby influences your behavior. Values also shape your beliefs in what is right or wrong, in what is good or bad. The society, which is also made up of the educational system, the current philosophies, the laws, religion and family culture, influences your values. When you know what you uphold and esteem as right and or as good, you will know how to control yourself and situations. Values protect your vision and ensure that you are not like a chaff blown to and fro, but that you are steadfast in your ways, whether it is good or bad. It is equally crucial to know the people around you and what visions and values they cherish.

8. Purpose: The Story of The Butterfly and The Eagle

"The greatest tragedy in life is not death, but a life without a purpose."

- Dr. Myles Munroe

The butterfly, as stated earlier on, starts its life's journey as a different species from what it finally becomes. The butterfly never questions the reason for its transformation process, but undergoes it and fulfils its function in the order of creation. It is not a matter of choice but an obligation, that is, its reason for existence. We all have a reason for existing, a function to fulfil and contribute to the good of all creation. Believe it or not, you have a role to play in this journey called life, despite your beginning. You might know how you began, but nobody, including you, knows how you will end.

Your purpose is your assignment here on earth, and it is the problem you are made to solve. There is no problem without a solution, therefore, you might be holding the solution to someone else's problem. The only issue is identifying that purpose and going through the process to Become. Without a vision, your purpose is not clear. Once your vision is clear, you will start to identify the assignments you can be a solution to. Without a purpose, you become unstable and ineffective.

PROCESS IS THE REFINING FIRE

I believe that no one is completely helpless or lost. We have the inherent capacity to decide the way forward for ourselves. It is the choice each of us must make. No matter the circumstances of your birth, and what you have been through or going through, I believe we all

have a place and a function to fulfill. As mentioned earlier, my ordeals made me question the very purpose of my existence. What good is living if all I get is pain?

Despite the harshness and noises of the world, there was a tiny voice within me that I held on to. The voice kept telling me not to give up. Though at first, this inner voice came in the form of fear, but somehow, it kept me desiring more of life and gave me hope. It also kept me curious, and at the end, it helped me to navigate through life. As I grew more in my faith, I came to identify this voice as my companion and helper, a gift from my Creator. This voice helped me come to terms with the hidden words within me.

The process is not an easy one, but that is the price you must be willing to pay to Become. If the caterpillar decided not to go through the process of transformation to become a new and better species, we would be deprived of its function and beauty.

The eagle also is a bird willing to undergo a painful transformation, to become a much stronger version of itself than it previously was. The eagle chooses a painful process of shedding its feathers to survive. This process

of rebirth lasts for about eight months, starting from the time of shedding of the old feathers to the growing of new ones. This process is very necessary because without it, the eagle will die. During this time, the eagle isolates itself on a high mountain to undergo this terrifying process which will allow it to live for another thirty more years. This is what makes the eagle the king of the birds.

Let's look at the metal called gold. Gold in its raw form is not beautiful and shiny. However, it must go through the refining fire to become pure, attractive, and valuable.

The process of Becoming is a painful one but very necessary. There are no shortcuts in this process. The shortcut mostly takes a longer route than the right process. You must be willing to look at yourself in the mirror and determine to battle through life, be ready to go through the process no matter how long or painful it takes to become your very best. Like Dr. Myles Munroe put it, *"You must decide if you are going to rob the world or bless it with the rich, valuable, potent, untapped resources locked away within you."*

Unlike the butterfly and the eagle, this process never ends. You must be willing to continually subject yourself to it, for each time you arise, you arise with more potentials which also need to be refined, tapped, and put into use.

YOUR GIFT WILL MAKE A WAY

Due to my experiences, I never thought I had anything to offer the world, I just wanted to live my life without failing. As I explained before, selfhatred had blindfolded me from seeing anything good in myself. I was living in my shadows, until I went through the process of uncovering the truth. Many of us are living like this. We live in our shadows at every stage of our lives, whereas, living life well needs the real us and the best of us. I had not thought of looking within me for the answers. I could not see anything good that could come out of me, because I saw myself as a broken vessel, and as an apple is trapped in a seed, so were and are my gifts trapped in me.

Your gift is that which you do with ease, that which comes natural to you. I believe we are all blessed with more than one gift since we have different roles to fulfill in life. Your gift is unique to you, meaning that no one can do it exactly the way you can. It is your signature. Your talents become clear when the purpose of your life is clear. However, it is important that you identify your purpose in life. It makes it easy for you to see the talents, abilities, and capabilities you have and those you need to develop to fulfill that purpose.

While growing up, whenever I was asked what I wanted to be in the future, my answer then was that I wanted to be a flight attendant. I couldn't remember how I got that idea because prior to that time, I had never even been closed to an airplane, nor had I been on one. However, the idea of being free like a bird and visiting different places was appealing to me and may have influenced me. As I grew older, this desire to be a flight attendant changed to that of being a lawyer, and then, to what I am now, a secondary school teacher and a mentor. All these desires were birthed from a place of a strong compulsion to help others become their best, especially the most vulnerable and the voiceless in society. My academic and career choices have been from the sincere desire to be at the service of others. Even now, this desire is as strong as ever. This book is because of this desire, which I consider to be my purpose in life.

I have this unwavering belief that there is greatness in each of us. We fail to see this because of the conditioning process we have been subjected to.

According to the societal model, we are taught to survive and take care of our basic needs first, before thinking of self-development, thus making the latter a luxurious commodity. I believe that our survival is intertwined with our self-development. You cannot survive and be fulfilled if you are living in your shadows. Discovering who you are, what your divine assignment is, what you have and how to fulfill it, is very necessary to your survival and that of the people around you. This is the principal thing in our lives, the order in nature.

The caterpillar that begins as a tiny egg and goes through all the processes to become a butterfly, does this because it has been programmed in its DNA to do so. We have also been created to become what we are destined to be, to transcend the modus of survival and thrive. It is important to note that talent development begins at an early age, and fortunately, that is what the Western world has come to realize and is now focusing on this aspect, even though there is still a long way to go.

Developing talents at an early age reduces the level of waste (talents) in the society, thereby increasing the general wealth as the individual's value and wealth grows.

Gifts and or talents come in different forms. Some folks are very good with handcrafts, painting, dancing, singing, acting, and such. While some are gifted with the ability to connect with people and understand them better, learn new things, adapt to different situations, and more. The truth is that, the more we serve others with our gifts, the more we improve on them. The problem is that we fail to recognize these gifts, instead, we admire those of others and want to be like them. We are all different because diversity is a blessing and is also a requirement. That is why there is so much diversity in nature. Every created thing carries out various functions in their uniqueness. I always use the analogy of the fingers. We all have five fingers on each hand. Each of these fingers has its own place and function. When one finger is missing, the others adapt and take the role of the finger that is no more, but it takes time for the others to adjust to this new reality. However, no matter how well the other fingers try to fill in the gap for the missing finger, the hand is not complete, because there is a disability on it. We are all equally important in this journey of life.

No matter how small you think you are, the solution you have for the other's problem is of great importance. For example, a clown makes people laugh and brings smiles to the faces of children and adults alike. That smile alone can give hope to that person. Another example is, a cleaner in an office. This person contributes to the cleanliness and beauty of the office. Without the cleaner in that office, how would that office look like?

So, it doesn't matter what your gifts are, what matters is that you recognize them, develop them where needed, put them to work, and continue to improve on them. You have the solution to either an existing problem or one yet to come, because, to every problem there is a solution. And even if there are existing solutions, that should not stop you from giving your own version of the solution. For as long as we all are different, we all have different tastes and are attracted to different things. Diversity is a blessing!

TRAGEDY OF WRONG USE OF GIFTS

You have unlimited potential in you. These potentials can manifest only if you are willing to discover them and use them efficiently. The people you are aspiring to be like, took time to go through the growing process and were willing to continue growing to achieve more. You and I pay them for the solutions they give us. Then why do you look at them and wish to be them? Why don't you look at their ethics and learn from those ethics that helped them be at their best? These ethics might help you become your best too. It is lamentable to be in a place you know you don't belong to. It is worse to be unaware that you are operating in the wrong place, in the wrong gift and vision, and it is equally tragic when you are aware of your gifts, yet choose to use them wrongly and selfishly. So instead of these gifts being a blessing and beneficial to all, it becomes self-centered and self-seeking.

The gifts we have are for the service of other people in one way or the other, to make a difference in their lives no matter how small it is. However, it becomes pitiful if the gift is for you alone, for no one will even notice your existence.
We have been given talents so that both humans and all other creations can become their very best.

What you possess is needed in this present life, and not in the afterlife. The only thing that transcends life is the legacy you leave behind, that is, the vision that gave you a clearer understanding and guided you in fulfilling your purpose, and the gifts you used in accomplishing this. Vision, purpose, and gifts all work hand in hand. How you go about it is what determines the duration of the vision and the quality of the result.

9. Strategies to Become

"The best way to predict the future is to create it."

- Abraham Lincoln

When people are faced with adversities, some of them retreat to think of a way to approach these adversities.

They examine all the options available to them and choose what they assume to be the most suitable one for them. Take the sports sector for example. During competitions, the competing parties map out ways and means to reach their goal, which is winning. They choose the players needed, they map out how they will play, when they will play, and where the event will take place. Furthermore, they anticipate the reaction of the opponents. The athletes are trained and coached according to all these analyses. The same strategies are applied when nations are at war. Before a country goes to war, extensive preparations are made. Without this, the soldiers sent to war will be in complete ignorance, and this will lead to defeat because they will have no idea what to expect nor how to respond. Nonetheless, as human beings, we cannot prepare for every situation. Having this in mind during every preparation, however, gives room for flexibility and adaptation.

Unfortunately, most people prepare only when faced with adversities. Preparation is very crucial, it is the key to either success or failure. Preparation is the mapping out of strategies and provides explanation to the 'how', the 'when', the 'who' and the 'where', including the 'what-ifs', assuming the 'why' and the 'what' are already known.

Many people skip this stage because it is a very tedious one that requires time and attention, whereas it is the key to victory. You can have the best vision and know your purpose and your gifts, but if you don't plan and act on them, the vision will remain what it is; a dream. Faith without works is dead!

The next section of this book is on the importance of strategy, it includes planning and other factors at our disposal that we can use wisely to achieve the desired goals.

ANY PLAN IS NOT A PLAN

I once had a plan with no vision, a plan to take life as it came. The only problem was that it made me unprepared for almost everything. I allowed fear to lead and to dictate my life. However, I realized soon enough that that was no plan at all. Every journey demands a careful plan. Waking up one day and deciding to go on a road trip without mapping out the destination can be good for a short time, but cannot be sustainable in the long run. The excitement can only last for a short while, but afterwards, the fun wears off and reality sinks in.

However, not to be misunderstood, I know that not everything in life can be planned. This is because even though planning is very important, there are unforeseen circumstances that can happen which we are not prepared for. An example are the people we come across. Sometimes, we don't know them beforehand, but it is essential we adjust ourselves to them, bearing our vision and purpose in mind. Planning, just like vision and values, gives us direction on the right path, and helps to keep our vision alive. But planning alone is not enough. In addition to planning, we must have the right mindset and values. Athletes, who thwart the plans of the coach, or who don't follow the guidelines of the game, neither do they have the discipline to endure the stress, are already defeated even before the game begins. Along with planning, we must have the right attitude and morals such as responsibility, determination, diligence, persistence, honesty, loyalty, discipline, and so on. The truth is, if we are not loyal to ourselves, we cannot be loyal to other people. We cannot be for others what we aren't ourselves. It must start from us before it can have a ripple effect on others.

THE TIME FACTOR

One essential factor of life often overlooked or taken for granted is TIME. In life, time is not bound to a place or a group of people. It is that which brings us all together, no matter where we are in the world. We all have a day we were born, and we will also die someday. The issue is that we don't all have the same time. While some people might have what looks like eternity, others might not have a quarter of that time to live. So, life therefore, is not measured in longevity, but in effectiveness. And just like the adage that says, *"it is not how long, but how well,"* no one knows how long they have to live, and since we all have 24 hours in a day, we also have the right to choose how to use it. The difference between a fulfilled life and a wasted life is in the use of time.

Time manifests in different ways. It is expressed in seconds, minutes, hours, days, weeks, months, years, age, seasons, decennia, centuries, millennia and so on. Time is infinite, but because it is captured in sequences in the finite, it becomes predictable, measurable, and sustainable. Time gives meaning and balance to life, and makes life predictable. Seasons, hours, and all the things about time are predictable. According to Jim Rhone's sayings, *"after the winter comes spring, before the fall, summer,"* farmers depend on this time system to sow and harvest, in regards to the natural system of farming. Every created thing has the notion of time implanted in them. For example, during the summer, ants gather food and store them in preparation for the winter period. But unlike other creatures who follow and use time instinctively, time is offered to us, humans, as a gift.

TIME IS A GIFT

As previously stated, time is infinite, yet it is finite to us due to the limited time of existence we have on earth. Note that before we were born, there were others who existed before us and as some of them have died, so also will we die when our time comes, but despite this, time will still continue.

Time is framed to give us guidance so that we can know when to do certain things and when to refrain, when to prepare a land for sowing and when to harvest and so on. Until I became aware of time, it was just me passing by. I wasted time in the form of procrastination, mediocrity, and being busy doing nothing. It is true that you can be busy doing a lot of things, and still be ineffective. That was how I was living life, very busy all the time, but not as effective as I should have been. I was happy with just getting things done, but procrastinate when the things were not needed at that time. There was always an excuse on why something was not done on time and I felt overwhelmed by it on most occasions. That was a wrong approach to time. Time is like the will; it is a gift given to us to use for our benefit and the benefit of others. In every new day, month, and year, are given opportunities to move you closer to your destiny. How you use this gift will determine how long your vision will live on after you are no more. For, we all have a beginning and an end, and there is time for everything as the wisest man that ever lived wrote in Ecclesiastes in the Bible.

Time is a currency used in exchange for something. So, if it is a currency, then it means that whatever you spend your energy on, you pay with time. The thing with currency is that, whenever you use it, it is gone, you cannot get that same amount of currency back. You only get the worth of what you valued it for. This is true about everything we pay for. You don't pay for an item or service just for nothing, but for the value of it. Whatever amount you are willing to pay for something is the worth of that thing for you. Some of us work very hard to get the necessary resources to purchase what we need and or desire, because we are not all equally blessed with these resources. Time, however, is the only thing everyone has equally. We all have twenty-four hours in a day, and it is necessary to know how to manage and use this time well to get the desired result. Moreover, we become what we spend our time on. When we have a better understanding of this, we can use time effectively to yield the best results for us.

Categories of Time

I have come to identify four categories of time users, they are: **time-wasters**, **time-consumers**, **time managers** and **time commanders**.

Time-wasters are those who use their time to do nothing that adds value to their lives. They waste time on unnecessary things, like movies, games, endless chatting and resting, and so on. They are not conscious of the value of time. They desire greatness but are either unwilling or unaware of their role in the process. Every year, they find themselves at the same spot with life. They are ignorant of the truth that they become whatever they exchanged their time for. And since a farmer who sows corn cannot harvest wheat because it is against the law of nature, so also, this group of people cannot expect to reap what they did not sow. They gradually transform to that which they have been exchanging their valued gift of time for. This happens automatically, a natural transformation according the principle of time.

This category of people always wants quick fix, they want to make it, but are unwilling to pay the price for that which they want. They have a misconception of the notion of time and value. Time wasters lack vision and purpose and most of them don't have any clear value to guide them.

Next are the **time-consumers**. They are endlessly busy with all kinds of things, which unfortunately are not producing good results. They also desire greatness and are tirelessly trying to get there. They have the knowledge of time, but lack the understanding of the value of it. They always never have time and seem to be overwhelmed by too many activities. They end up being ineffective due to inappropriate use of time. They forget, hereby, that time spent, is time gone and whatever you spend it on, is what you will get later.

The third group are **time managers**. These are people who manage time effectively. Like effective managers, they approach time as something they can have a level of control over and use it for their benefit. This category of time users understand that time is a currency, and they plan their lives with this knowledge.

They prioritize their work in such a way that, anything considered as time consuming with little outcome, is not given priority, or they look for other ways to do it differently within their desired time-frame. They understand that investing wisely in productive work will give them the best out of time and increase their gain. They understand the law of time which states that, "whatever you don't invest on, will not yield for you." A farmer that fails to invest by sowing the right seeds in the right season, cannot expect to reap during the harvest time.

Lastly, the final category is a special group, one I have come to identify as the **time commanders**. I call them time commanders, not because they command time, but because they have a level of mastery over the law of time. Although, time cannot be controlled by any human hands, this group has found a way to submit themselves to time while using it to their advantage.

Like the children of Issachar in the Bible, they can discern time and all its seasons through their knowledge and mastery of it. To them, time is not static, but a dynamic force that can be predicted and used at the right moment. Because of their level of knowledge and understanding, they work in wisdom and get good outcomes due to the good use of their time. They are like the eagle that uses the storm to rest its wings while still focusing on the goal

Like the eagle, they are ready to go into isolation and undergo the process of shedding off old feathers to come out gloriously, no matter how long it might take them. They have a good understanding of what time entails, so this makes them to approach it not according to hours or days, but according to seasons. They bend time and its outcome and because of this, time seems to be on their side, making them effective in most of their endeavors.

To other people, this category of time users seems to have everything working for them because of the results they yield. The efforts and hard work they put into place and maintained to get to the top are mostly ignored or not recognized.

Very few people in every generation attain this level of mastery over time, because most of us are unwilling to put in the work to attain this level. It requires an intense, disciplined, diligent and deliberate investment of time to reach this level. It also requires submission to the principles governing time before one can understand it and work in perfect harmony with it.

Reflect on these four categories and see where you belong. I used to belong to the first two categories, time-wasters and time-consumers. I am still finding a balance in the third category as a time-manager, but it requires intentional and conscious decisions. My aspiration is to persevere, aiming to become a time commander, because this is the most effective use of time in all its ramifications. I invite you to join me in this.

As free beings, time is at our disposal, to serve us, not for us to serve it, because if we serve it, we put ourselves into bondage.

As you become more conscious of time, you must learn to manage it well by planning your days, weeks, and years to get more out of it. As mentioned before, we all have twenty-four hours in a day. What differentiates one person from the other is the effective use of these hours.

THE PHANTOM OF SUCCESS

Like many of us, I thought success was being rich and being at the top, because society makes it feel like that. Even at home, among peers, someone is always compared with the other. That always gives a feeling of never being good enough, because the rival is always better than the other in these comparisons. As I grew up and matured, I found out that the indicators we use for success are misleading. After reading *Think and Grow Rich* and *The Law of Success*, books written by Napoleon Hill and other books on this subject, my concept and understanding of success changed. I came to realize that life is not a battle or a competition between people, but a battle with one's self, and since it is a battle within, success cannot be outside of the individual. Success is therefore already inbuilt in the self. It is however, dependent on

external forces or influences to become complete.

There is a collaboration from outside of self needed for one to become successful.

Let us take the story of the apple tree as an example. The seed of the apple contains both the tree and the fruit accordingly. If the seed grows into a tree, but the tree is unable to produce fruits, then both the seed and the tree have failed in their purpose. The fruit is the gift of the seed to nature, which in return multiplies the seeds, thus bearing more fruits.

For the apple tree to yield the necessary fruits for nature, nature must produce the elements the seed and the tree needs, like water and the sun. This is where nature and nurture from human hands collaborate to make things work accordingly. Without this collaboration, the success of the apple seed and tree will be impossible. That is the same for us. Our success is hidden in us, not outside of us. Just like the tree and the fruit are in the seed, so also our potentials are in us. We must strive to develop these potentials every day, but we cannot do this without the help of nature and without the intentional decision to Become. That is what differentiates us from all other creatures; the freedom of choice. This choice makes all the difference in how a person successfully uses time while the other gets stuck in it.

The Quest for Greatness

Every living thing, whether human or animal, has the desire to be great because it is inbuilt in them. This is what makes the caterpillar retreat and undergo the transformation process into a butterfly. This is also the reason why the eagle submits itself to the painful process of shedding off old feathers, with the purpose of coming out greater and stronger than before. Same goes for us as human beings. We compete out of the desire for greatness. Intuitively, we know we weren't born to just eat, sleep and die, but that we are destined for greatness. The issue is that most of the time, we fail to see what it demands and are unwilling to submit to the principles or conditions necessary to achieve this greatness. That is why most of us approach life as if it is a competition, assuming that it is the way to attain greatness. This is, however, a wrong approach. As explained in the previous sections of this book, life is a journey and not a race or a competition with others. It is a quest to find our true selves. Out of this quest for greatness, many have followed different kinds of doctrines and have adopted all kinds of values to shape their lives and surroundings. They seek to dominate their environment to justify it as having attained greatness. Having dominion over others is never and should never be the parameter for greatness, rather, it is dominion over nature and time in relation to self.

Greatness is the ability to actualize all your potentials and achieve your goals within your giving time-frame on earth. However, the level of your greatness can only be measured after you leave this world. That is when the balance is weighed and the conclusions drawn. Every step you take in the journey of life brings you closer to finding and achieving this greatness. That is why you never stop learning and developing till you exit this world. The moment you stop learning, you stop growing, and

stop moving forward but backwards. That is against both the spiritual law and the law of nature.
That is why slothfulness is such a danger to our progress.

Slothfulness is best defined as refusing to be meaningful or being ignorant of your talents and gifts, and therefore not being effective in your assignment in life. Time and resources are wasted because of ignorance or the refusal to be relevant. Slothful people are the greatest timewasters, they short-change themselves and society at large by withholding their gifts.

To be great, one must be willing to put in the work, to go through the process and become successful, hereby working in perfect harmony with time.

Failure as Success

Thomas Edison, one of America's and the world's greatest mind, is an example of success in every area. Edison did not finish or attend school for a long time. He was eager to find out how things worked by dismantling them and assembling them again. Edison worked very hard on all his inventions, failing many times before getting one breakthrough. One of his inventions was the light bulb. It is said that Edison had over a thousand attempts at this invention before he became successful. When he was asked why he continued after so many failures, he said, "*At least, I learned how not to do it each time I failed.*" He saw failure as not the end, but as another opportunity to try again in a different way. That was his key to success. Edison himself was said to have had hearing problems, yet he invented the first phonograph, the machine that could record sound which is a great discovery for the music and movie industry. Edison was a genius who did not allow his circumstances to dictate to him but had mastery over them. He said the following words,

"A genius is 1% inspiration and 99% perspiration." Meaning that what made him successful were not the visions, and the dreams alone, but hard work, determination, and perseverance.

Failure was just another way to approach success. Albert Einstein, another genius, also said the following, *"The height of stupidity is doing the same thing over and over, expecting different results each time."* Failure is not the end but an opportunity to retreat, retrace and learn from the mistakes, and then try again. Many of us allow one failure to break us or hold us back. We allow the fear from that failure to stop us from trying again.

If Edison allowed his hearing problem, his background, and circumstances to stop him, we would probably not be enjoying most of his inventions today, or it might have come much later than then. Trying different ways to solve the same problem is not a waste of time, but an asset. Failure is failing to try!

Wisdom in Success

As written earlier, real success is not outside of one's self, but it is within the self. Competing with another person is a waste of time. We all have our roles to play in life. Some people see life as a race. Well, when you see life like that, then everything becomes a competition, because that is what a race is all about, a tournament where the winners are being rewarded, but the losers go home with nothing. This is not the essence of life.

I see life as a journey, because a journey has a different destination for everyone and therefore requires different approaches to get to that destination. It is a journey with multiple stops on the way, but only ends when the person dies.

When you see life like this instead of seeing it as a race, your attitude towards it will change. That is why the process for you to become never ends in this life.

Success can be limiting if not properly controlled. Some of us think we have succeeded in life after one achievement. This is one of the most dangerous things plaguing us in the process of Becoming. When we get a breakthrough in an aspect of our lives, we get so hooked on it that it becomes a limitation to our progress. An athlete who does not aim to break his previous record is simply preparing to fail. The success of yesterday was the glory of yesterday, it is history and therefore can only be stated as a reference.

Is your success of the past still making an impact today? If so, how is it affecting you? Have you improved on anything to make your present more impactful than your past or are you still feeding on that success? Feeding on yesterday's glory is like feeding on expired food. The freshness, brightness and impact diminish with the day if it is not continually sustained. Today is a new day with new opportunities and a new chance of success. "I was" is not the same as "I am". I was a big success back in the days is nothing if it does not reflect in your today.

The knowledge and understanding of the finite reality in the infinite time makes me humble in my approach to life. Success, to me, is a daily goal. I pray every day to be a blessing to others, no matter how little it might be. To this effect, I have developed the habit of self-reflection, because this is essential for self-improvement. Not that I am striving for perfection, I am just trying to be the best version of me, so that I can give my best because I believe I have much to offer. Initially, this reflection was done out of the fear of failure and rejection, but as I mature and grow in understanding, my motives for doing this have changed.

Making time to reflect on your actions, attitude, work and or character, helps you to identify those areas that need to be let go of to become a better person. Reflecting on my past and my present helps me to know how to move forward. If you have never taken out time to reflect on yourself, please, start making this a habit. You will be confronted with some hidden truths about yourself, but you will come out stronger and better prepared if you are open and honest to yourself during this process.

Success should be seen in the little achievements, but never have the mentality that you have accomplished your purpose in life because of a little breakthrough. The moment you do that, you block yourself from growing and reaching a true level of greatness. Every success is a stepping stone to the next one, a brick or ladder to use to the next level. Just as games are played in stages, so we also should approach life in stages, though not as a game, for life is not a game. However, life does come in different stages and must be treated as such.

Another thing I have identified as a stumbling block to success, apart from slothfulness, is Pride. Pride is an attitude that blocks a person from seeing further. It makes the person feel overly important, and to think that without him or her, nothing can be done or achieved. Pride is a limiting force to tomorrow's success because it blocks you from achieving or reaching your best today. Pride clouds you from seeing your potentials and from seeing that of others that will be of great help to you. Thomas Edison never stopped with one invention. Even on that one invention, he still found ways to improve, devising different versions of the same idea on every occasion. In a similar way, did many like him whom we refer to as epitome of greatness. We still refer to them because of the impact their inventions, theories and or ideas are still having today. That is what true greatness is.

We all have smartphones, iPad's, and others. Most of the Software and applications on them update regularly to function well. At regular times, updates are programmed and executed. There is someone or people working tirelessly behind the scenes to make these updates happen. We human beings are computers with brains and emotions. To function well and achieve greatness, we need to go beyond yesterday's success, update, and upgrade regularly to be ready to embrace tomorrow. Just as the onions have many layers, so also our potentials have many layers. Give yourself a little bit of a challenge each day to undergo the process to Become. Nonetheless, this process is not straightforward and never ends.

No Man is an Island

Being successful in life is also acknowledging that you are not alone in the journey. You cannot do it all alone. The architect of a building project does not only envision, but also plan and supervise the whole project. The builder is never left all by himself. Without the supervision of the architect, working hand in hand with the builder to ensure the success of the project, the builder might make a mistake which may lead to the collapse of the project. Moreover, the builder does not carry the burden of the project all alone, but surrounds himself with other capable and crafted co-workers to accomplish the task. Though each co-worker is specialized in his/her own field of work, it is only when they join their different talents together in one purpose that they become successful.

We need each other to become the very best of ourselves. Thomas Edison became great because he applied wisdom. Most of the inventions in his name came because he aligned himself with others who had the vision and the knowledge but lacked the skills or did not have the resources to make their vision a reality. Edison brought them in and worked with them. Whatever invention that came out of those collaborations, he patented them in his name. Edison had the vision, the resources, and where he lacked in knowledge, he made up for it by partnering or employing the right people. He became who he was also because he learned from others who were in his field of work before him and those around him. No man is an island. As much as success is a thing within one's self, it becomes complete when it is used correctly and effectively. On this journey, others are needed to help you, support you, challenge you, inspire you or even try to stop you.

Adversities should not discourage you but equip you not to give up no matter what. You should see adversities as the refining fire that refines you to bring the pure and shiny gold out of you. I experienced one of the most remarkable adversities in my life in my fourth year in Belgium. Until then,

I had a seemingly smooth transition from Ghana to Belgium, except for settling in in a new place and with a new person. My academics, however challenging, were going well. I had been in schools with people from diverse social and ethnic backgrounds, so this experience was very enriching. However, in my fourth year, I chose a different school to further my education. Some of my friends attended this school with me, but this school almost broke us all. For the very first time in my life, I hated school, the thought of it got me angry. We were invisible to the teachers and to other pupils. One teacher used to say that we were taking the place of those much deserving to be there, just because of our origins. We were friends from different countries: Bosnia, Morocco, Chile, Congo, and Ghana. We all had our dreams, but these dreams almost got shattered by the experiences we went through in that school. At one point, we started skipping classes by hanging out in the parks instead of the classroom. Most of us either received negative advice or did not pass that school year. Generally, the class council gives negative advice when they feel a student has been wrongly oriented to a higher course. Even though I passed my school year, I still received negative advice to go and do a vocational training course. But I made up my mind not to let them dictate my life. I knew I could do more than I did. So, instead of following the advice, I registered in a different school where I presented my results and chose the course I wanted. Though I was one year behind in that course, the school was willing to give

willing to give me a chance if I was willing to put in the work. Thanks to my faith in God and belief in the ability that I can really do better, I was able to turn the adversity around. Howbeit, racism and discrimination were at their best in that school and it left a deep mark in my heart.

People you meet along the way can be a stepping stone, a challenge to overcome, or a hindrance to avoid. They will undoubtedly impact your life one way or the other. The stronger your character,

knowledge and understanding in your purpose and in the
mystery of time, the more prepared you will be to handle the situations and people that present themselves to you.

CONCLUSION

The journey of life is an individual assignment that only you can make it happen.

This journey is a process that requires you to Become by discovering who you are. Only you can answer the question of who you are, because any other attempt will only be a reflection or a shadow of the real you. In this journey, you will need to go back to trace the monsters still influencing your present from your past. The keys to the seemingly closed doors in your life are not far from you, but you must strip off the mask layer by layer to stop the powers hindering you to Become.

The great Architect has already designed your life and handed it over to you. Like a builder, you are to understand the mechanisms and characteristics of the design for you to be able to build it. You will meet people and circumstances along the way that will either help you or hinder your progress.

It is equally important to identify the emotions that affect you and how they do. Emotions, as we know, are powerful. We are wired with emotions because they are necessary for our survival. However, the inappropriate use of them or the lack of the ability to control them can be a hindrance to your progress. The will is a strong emotion. It is a gift to be used wisely. The will, if untamed, can lead to chaos both to the individual and to society. Nevertheless, you have the choice on how to use this gift from the Creator. Whatever you choose to do or not to do, make sure to test it with the law of nature and the spiritual law, considering that right is not good, and good is not right. What is good to you is based on your perceptions, values, or philosophy and this is not necessarily the case for the person next to you. However, right is universal and cannot change.

The process to become can be painful and time consuming sometimes. But if you are willing to go through the process of transformation like the butterfly and the eagle, you can never Become and release the hidden treasures in you. Moreover, you will be denying all creation from your gifts. You are an earthen vessel endowed with hidden potentials that the rest of creation need since we are all interdependent. The failure of one is the failure of all. That is how significant you are. The only thing stopping you is how you see yourself and what you are willing to do to Become.

To Become and therefore, to be successful in life and achieve greatness, you must also understand how things work and apply wisdom in all your choices.

Above all, use Time to your benefit instead of serving it. Your attitude, and your character is crucial in this whole process. There is an adage that says, *"Your attitude determines your altitude,"* that is very true. Your character opens or closes doors for you, because your character reflects in all your works. Abraham Lincoln said, *"Nearly all men can stand adversity, but if you want to test a man's character, give him power."* He also said, *"Character is like a tree and reputation like a shadow. The shadow is what we think of it, the tree is the real thing."* Character, no matter how long-hidden, will always surface. Instead of trying to cover it up, why not take time and work it out?

Build a strong and healthy character with a vision worthy of emulating. Let it be one that gives no room for slothfulness and pride but seeks to serve others. Your vision must be powerful enough to transcends both the present and the future.

NOTES

SCRIPTURE REFERENCES

1 For the creation waits in eager expectation for the children of God to be revealed. Romans 8:19 (NIV). pp. 39 & 86

2. The story of the Sower is about Isaac, who sowed in the time of drought. He sowed against all odds, facing multiple challenges: the drought and hostility from the surrounding people. Genesis 26:1 – 13 (NIV). p. 43

3. Faith is defined in the Bible as the confidence in what we hope for and assurance about what we do not see. Hebrews 11:1 (NIV). p. 100

4. Faith without works is dead is derived from the following Bible verse: Even so faith, if it hath not works, is dead, being alone. James 2:17 King James Version (KJV). p. 118

5. The book of Ecclesiastes is written by King Solomon, son of King David. He wrote "there is time for everything, and a season for

every activity under the heavens." Ecclesiastes 3:1 (NIV). p. 123

6. The children of Issachar are said to have unusual gift over time. They could decipher time and knewexactly when Israel should do. 1 Chronicles 12:32 (NIV). p. 126

SOCIETAL MODEL

7. Societal model is a reference to the Pyramid of Maslow, also referred to as Maslow's hierarchy of needs by Abraham Maslow. The hierarchy of needs classifies human needs into 5 categories, with the basics of needs being psychological and biological needs (food, shelter, clothing, etc.). Self-actualization is at the top of the pyramid. According to this model, the basic needs must first be satisfied before one can be motivated to move to the next need in line. The leading economic model in the world today is

predominantly built on this theory. Self-actualization is the preferred modus operandi; however, it can only be achieved when other needs are satisfied. p. 112

REFERENCES

Adichie, C. N. (2009). The danger of a single story. *TEDGlobal 2009.* TED Conference Retrieved 01-06-2020, from https://www.ted.com/talks/chimamanda_ngozi_adichie_the_danger_of_a_single_story

Dr. Munroe, M. (2005). *The Spirit of Leadership.* United States of America: Whitaker House.

Everyday Power. (n.d.). Choices and Concequnces *Quotes.* Retrieved 19-11-2021 from https://everydaypower.com/quotes-aboutchoices-and-consequences/

Gianoutsos, J. (2006). Locke and Rousseau: Early Childhood Education. *The Pulse, Issues, Vol. 4, No 1,Falls 2006.* Baylor University. Retrieved 02-07-2020, from https://www.baylor.edu/pulse/index.php?id=42091

Grice, E. (2006). *Cry of an Enfant Sauvage.* Retrieved 17-10-2020, from The Telegraph: https://www.telegraph.co.uk/tv/0/cryenfant-sauvage/

Hernandez, R. (2017). The Biograpghy of Thomas Edison. Createspace Independent Publishing Platform.

Hill, N. (2017). Think & Grow Rich. Indirapuram, Ghziabad: Samaira Book Publishers.

Hill, N. (2018). The Law of Success. Indirapuram, Ghaziabad: Samaira Book Publishers.

Maslow, H. A. (1954). *Motivation and Personality.* New Yourk City, NY, USA: Harper and Row.

Rohn, J. (1997). *Leading An Inspired Life.* Niles, Illinois, USA: Nightingale-Conant Corporation.

Rowan, L. (sd). *Oxana Malaya: The Story of a Girl Raised by Dogs.* Retrieved 05-04-2022, from History Daily: https://historydaily.org/oxana-malaya-story-girlraised-dogs

The Forbiden Experiment. (2013). (WNYC Studios)

Retrieved 03-12-2020, from Radiolab: https://radiolab.org/episodes/293679-forbiddenexperiment

CPSIA information can be obtained
at www.ICGtesting.com
Printed in the USA
BVHW010833200423
662716BV00021B/754

9 789464 665703